The Call for Independence

★☆★☆★☆★☆★☆★☆★☆★☆★☆★☆★☆★☆★☆★☆★☆★☆★☆★☆★☆★

The Story of the American Revolution and Its Causes

The Call for

The Story of the

☆☆☆☆☆☆☆☆☆☆☆☆☆☆☆☆☆☆☆☆☆☆☆☆

Independence

American Revolution and Its Causes

☆☆☆☆☆☆☆☆☆☆☆☆☆☆☆☆☆☆☆☆☆☆

Stephen Meyeroff

OAK TREE PUBLISHERS

Copyright © 1996 by Stephen Meyeroff
Library of Congress Card Catalog number 95-070366
cloth edition ISBN 0-9646602-0-2
paper edition ISBN 0-9646602-1-0

Oak Tree Publishers
P.O. Box 345
Cherry Hill
New Jersey 08003-0345

Designed by Adrianne Onderdonk Dudden

First Printing 1996

To Robyn—
my wife, my friend, my love,
whose support, encouragement and help,
made this book possible.

Contents

Part Two The War for Independence

Introduction

This book is designed to give the student of American history a solid foundation in the causes leading up to the American Revolution and the war itself. It is not a cold list of events. Instead each cause leading to the split between Britain and its American colonies is carefully analyzed and put into perspective for the times. Many of the Acts passed by Parliament may seem ludicrous by today's standards; yet in colonial America they may have been believed to be proper. Only by explaining the actions of both sides in the conflict and by showing how each action affected both sides can the student not only learn about the events which led to war but understand them as well.

Part One

The Causes Which Led to War

Setting the Stage

★☆★☆★☆★☆★☆★☆★☆★☆★☆★☆★☆★☆★☆

The captain who was preparing three ships for his expedition could never have imagined how his voyage would change the future of the world. Setting sail from Spain in the summer of 1492, Columbus began an adventure. By the fall of the same year, Columbus discovered America. It was really more of a find than a discovery. For well over 14,000 years, Indians had known about the Americas and had lived there. From the top of North America to the tip of South America, including the islands of the Caribbean, many different Indian nations and cultures flourished.

When Columbus returned to Europe with news of his belief that he had reached India, the life that the American Indian tribes had known was about to change. Fifteen years would pass from the time of Columbus' first voyage before the Europeans realized that they had not reached Asia, but instead landed on two continents previously unknown to them.

Once the Europeans understood that "a new world" had been discovered, they rushed to grab as much of it as possible. Ignoring the rights of the Indian people who inhabited the lands, the Europeans claimed territories of their own.

There were three European nations that became the major colonial powers over the Americas.

Spanish Colonization   First came the Spanish who claimed lands by virtue of Columbus' voyages. Since Columbus was the first European to go there and return with knowledge of the lands existence, Spain figured it should own the Americas. The King and Queen of Spain had paid for Columbus' expeditions in the hope of finding riches. Originally, they hoped Columbus' voyages would enable them to control the spice trade from the Far East. If Spain could do this, it would become a rich nation. Once the Spanish realized that they had not found a new route to India, they proceeded to try to establish control over the Americas.

Spain was a very religious Catholic country and decided that it was their duty as a Christian nation to take over the savage Indians, control their lands, and convert them to Christianity. The Spanish government sent soldiers and missionaries to the Americas. Missionaries were the religious leaders who tried to convert the Indians to Christianity. While in the process of converting the Indians, Spain felt it was all right if it became wealthy in the process.

Soon, Spain's main objective was to collect valuables such as gold and rare jewels. In its search for wealth, Spain colonized Mexico, Central and South America and many of the islands in the Caribbean. The North American coastline was left largely untouched.

The Spanish attitude toward the Indians set the pattern for the Americas. Spain would take over the lands by force, enslaving and using the Indians as it decided. The Spanish government also decided that it was all right to steal the Indian treasures and send them to Spain. Believing they were doing their duty, Spanish missionaries destroyed as much of the Indian cultures as they could. They always tried to replace the destroyed portion of the Indian culture with Christianity. To the Europeans who came to America, it was their culture that had value; the Indians culture was worthless and should be destroyed.

The Spanish soldiers who came, were in the "new world" for many years at a time and so Spain allowed them to marry Indian natives. A culture with two social levels quickly developed. The Spanish ruled while the Indians worked. The children of the marriages between the soldiers and Indians were Indian under Spanish law.

Shiploads of Spanish came, but they were soldiers and missionaries. Searching for gold or working for God, they did not come to stay and build a new society. Most came to search for wealth and then hoped to return with their found treasures to Spain.

The Spanish colonies existed under a cruel system, which brutalized the natives. For the Spanish, an Indian life was without any value.

While many Indians died because of Spanish cruelty, many more died because of disease. As the first Europeans came to the Americas, they carried with them diseases for which the Indians had no resistance. Entire tribes were wiped out in just a few short years after coming into contact with the Europeans. Colds, flu, measles, and mumps killed off entire tribes in just a short time. Between the diseases and cruelty, it was no wonder that the Indians quickly learned to hate and distrust the Europeans.

French Colonization

France was the second major European power to venture into the Americas. Like the Spanish, they did not come to create permanent settlements. However, instead of conquering the Indians as the Spanish did, the French came as friends wanting to trade with the Indians. They wanted the furs which the Indians were able to trap. In turn, the French gave the

Indians the things they wanted and needed. The French explored the eastern portion of Canada, south down along the Mississippi River, and its surrounding areas. They too brought missionaries, but the French missionaries did not attempt to destroy the Indian cultures; they merely wanted to convert the Indians to Christianity.

The French changed the nature of many of the North American Indian tribes. The Indians went from self sufficient cultures, in which they made everything they needed and used, to ones that depended on foreign trade for survival. Once the Indians became used to hunting with muskets, they became dependent on the Europeans for guns, powder, and lead for bullets. The North American Indians' way of life was forever changed.

For the most part, the French left the Indians alone, establishing only a few forts and trading posts. Boatloads of French citizens never came to conquer the Indians. Although French colonies were established in America, they never really grew large. The small showing in North America left the French weak in the new world.

English Colonization The last major European power to come to the Americas was England. England had been a small island nation in Europe, but after a war with Spain and the defeat of the Spanish Armada (navy) in the middle of the sixteenth century, England became a major naval power.

In the late 1500's and early 1600's, the English explored and then claimed the Atlantic coastal areas which were to the south of the French and to the north of the Spanish colonies. Now with England in the colonial game, things were about to change.

The English Colonies Are Established

★☆☆☆☆☆☆☆☆☆☆☆☆☆☆☆☆☆☆☆☆☆☆☆

The English used the Americas far differently than did the other European nations. The colonies established by the English were not for conquest of the Indians nor to solely create Indian trade. The English colony was a permanent settlement created with the hope of growth and development.

The English colonist came to build a home and a new life. With him came women and children and livestock for farms. Often the initial settlement was a business venture established through the king by a royal charter. The companies which began a colony did so in the hope that the colony would grow and create products to be sent to England. Through this trade the company would make a profit. By using the company process, a settlement could be started on land given by the king.

In the early 1600's, the first English settlement was attempted in Virginia. Weather, Indians, and a lack of planning helped to doom the first attempts. After the first few tries at creating a colony, a successful permanent settlement was established in Jamestown, Virginia in 1607.

The people who came to the new lands were adventurous, knowing that they would be 3,000 miles away from England. Instead of having the comfort of friends and family, they would be alone on a different continent. This spirit of adventure brought a hard working, independent individual, willing to take risks. The land was suitable for people with that kind of spirit.

The first colony was established by the Virginia Company. This business venture hoped to make a profit through the trade of the colonists' farm produce. In the beginning, the company decided it was going to run all the aspects of the colony, but found it too difficult to do. The Virginia Company was unable to oversee the day to day life of the colony from faraway England. Within a few years of the first settlement, the House of Burgesses was authorized in Virginia.

The House of Burgesses, established in 1619, became the legislative body which met with the Royal Governor to discuss the laws and administration of the Virginia colony. The colony itself was divided into districts and a representative from each district was elected to the House of Burgesses. The Virginia Company was not obligated to go by their recommendations but almost always did. Quickly the House of Burgesses, along with the Royal Governor, became the sole source of laws and regulations for the colony.

In 1624, the Royal Charter, which had been given to the Virginia Company, was revoked. The colony became the personal property of the King of England. The Royal Governor was now in charge of the colony by appointment of the King. At the time Virginia was being made the King's property, it was also developing its own legal system. In 1624, Virginia established jury trials to deal with law breakers. The colony had decided that 12 men should be selected for a jury to make decisions of guilt or innocence. Women were not part of the political system and were therefore not allowed to serve.

A representative government had been established in Virginia. Like the company before, the Royal Governor did not have to listen to the recommendations of the legislature, but most often did. A tradition of legislative control in the colony had begun.

These actions which occurred in Virginia would create a pattern for other colonies to come. Even before a second colony was

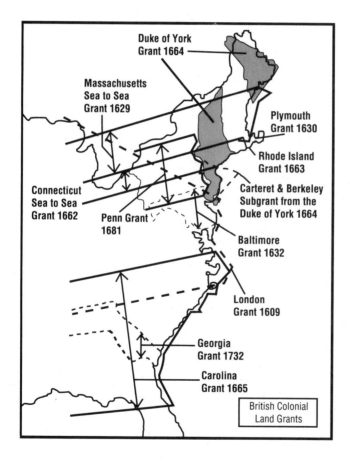

Duke of York
Grant 1664

Massachusetts
Sea to Sea
Grant 1629

Plymouth
Grant 1630

Rhode Island
Grant 1663

Connecticut
Sea to Sea
Grant 1662

Carteret & Berkeley
Subgrant from the
Duke of York 1664

Penn Grant
1681

Baltimore
Grant 1632

London
Grant 1609

Georgia
Grant 1732

Carolina
Grant 1665

British Colonial
Land Grants

established, representative government and colonial courts had found a foothold in the English colonies.

The Northern Colonies Not all who came to the "new world" came for fortune and opportunity. In the early 1600s, religion and government were intertwined to the point that they were often the same thing. In England, the official religion was the Anglican Church, referred to as the Church of England. Although not a Catholic nation like Spain, England wanted all of its citizens to be members of the Church of England and follow the dictates of the Church. But not all the people wanted to follow the Anglican Church!

The Puritans were a religious sect who practiced religion differently from the Church of England. Forced to flee England to practice religion in the way of their own choosing, they first went to Holland. There they found a moment of freedom but this too was temporary and they were again forced to make another move. The King of England, along with several businessmen, saw a great opportunity here.

These religious troublemakers would be allowed to go to the new world and start their own colony. England would get a double benefit. First it would get rid of the people it did not want, while at the same time profits could be made from the colony they would establish.

In 1620, a ship bound for Virginia was fully loaded with Pilgrim troublemakers. The Pilgrims were a group of Puritans who searched for a better place and way of living. The ship, the *Mayflower*, was intentionally set off course by the captain under instructions from England. When they finally reached North America, the Puritans found that they were not in Virginia, where they expected to arrive. The *Mayflower* landed in Massachusetts, at Plymouth, far to the north of Virginia.

England thus established its second colony.

Realizing that they were far from where they had intended to be, the Pilgrim leaders gathered together before leaving the ship and created the Mayflower Compact. A simple document, the Mayflower Compact established the laws and rules of life for the newly formed Bay Colony. These colonists had created a written constitution. They had made their own laws.

It was a new idea—ordinary men inventing and then participating in their own government!

The Pilgrims came for religious freedom. They wanted freedom to practice religion in their own manner. But the government they created was not much different from the one in England. Anyone could come to live in the Pilgrim's colony, so long as he/she was willing to practice religion the Pilgrims' way. They were just as intolerant as the King from whom they had fled, and they did not offer freedom of religion to others.

The Pilgrims established the Plymouth Colony. The Puritans, who followed also went to the north but established their own colony nearby the Pilgrims.

The Massachusetts Bay Colony directly held its own charter from the King. There was no company created as in Virginia. Holding its own charter made the Bay Colony, as it was called, a self-governing colony. The freemen of the colony were able to select their own Governor and his Council, and elect representatives to the General Court, which was the assembly or legislative body for the colony.

From the very beginning, Massachusetts experienced a high degree of independence from England. Additional religious leaders came with more people. The Bay Colony grew and prospered.

In 1629, an economic depression gripped England. With hard times, many people were forced to escape the poverty and troubles of England and were willing to try to survive the hardships required to come to the new world.

The new world offered promise and hope. Farmland was very difficult to get in England, but America had an endless amount of land. Hard work to clear the land would provide every man a chance for a good farm. Wild game in the forests would provide food for a family. From the beginning, America promised to be the land of opportunity.

And so they came, by the shiploads.

☆☆

In 1636, the Reverend Thomas Hooker established Hartford and thus the colony of Connecticut was begun. Again, like the Bay Colony, Reverend Hooker helped draft a constitution, the Fundamental Orders, which gave the right to vote to all free men, not just church members. Expanding the right to vote and to participate in the government was the next step in the process of creating a democratic government. But it was just one more step; there were many more to come.

☆☆

At the same time that Reverend Hooker was settling in Hartford, things in the Bay Colony were not going smoothly. Roger Williams, one of the many religious leaders who came to the colony, protested the Bay Colony's control of church and state. He believed that the government and the church should be separated. He was also angry about the way the colonists cheated the Indians and took away their land. He demanded that the Indians be treated fairly. Those in authority in the Bay Colony were shocked. How dare Williams challenge them and the way they chose to do things?

Forced to leave the colony in 1636, Roger Williams led others who felt as he did and founded Providence in Rhode Island. The concept of separation of church and state had now been established in the colonies.

☆☆

Things were beginning to change. Next came a challenge to the way the Bay Colony interpreted religion. The leaders of the colony were also the religious leaders and they determined how the religion was to be practiced. Any ideas they did not agree with were not to be tolerated.

In a time when women had no say in their church and government, Anne Hutchinson led a protest against the leaders of her community. She believed each individual had the right to interpret the Bible his or her own way and led a protest in the Bay Colony over the way its leaders interpreted their religion. The force of her convictions and the will of her strength opened the door for others to follow her. Her loose view of religion, which allowed the individual more say in the practice of religion, caused Hutchinson to be banished from the Bay Colony. With her followers, she moved to an area near Providence, where they began a colony of their own. Again, another colony was established through protest. Allowing colonists to be independent was paying off for England.

Whether by design or circumstances, the English colonies were growing and expanding. The English colonists felt it was all right to speak up and protest when they believed themselves to be in the right. This was setting the pattern for protests which were to come.

☆☆

In 1632, the King gave a grant of land, named Maryland, to Lord Baltimore, George Calvert. Maryland, settled by Lord Baltimore, was created for individuals with the same religious preference as his. Once again, another colony was begun because of an individual willing to express his own desires and beliefs.

Calvert's colony did poorly in the beginning and so to attract more people to the colony, Lord Baltimore decided to give land and a say in the rule of the colony to individuals who would come to his colony. The 1649 Toleration Act of Maryland gave to anyone of any religious sect who professed to believe in Christ the right to settle. All Christian sects were welcomed no matter how they practiced their religion. A say in the government, free land, and more religious freedom opened up Maryland to new settlers.

The year 1643 saw a new advancement in the northern colonies. The New England Confederation of Colonies was established. Massachusetts, Plymouth, Connecticut, New Haven, and Rhode Island all agreed to a mutual defense treaty from Indians. Although independent and separate, some of the colonies had begun to realize that they faced certain common problems. They decided that by working together, their problems could be handled. For the first time, and on their own, the English colonies in North America chose to establish an agreement with other colonies. Although quite limited in the amount of cooperation between colonies, it did set a precedent for mutual cooperation.

☆☆

In what may be called a bloodless war, in 1664, the British took the Dutch colony of New Holland. It was renamed New York.

Even before the British came, religious conflict developed in New Holland. In 1655, Jews had come to the colony and wanted to build a synagogue to practice their own religion. The Dutch East Trading Company, which ran the colony, suggested they construct their own colony alongside the colony which had been established. This was an attempt to separate the different groups. Many of the Dutch Jews refused to do this and decided to move to the Caribbean Island of Barbados, where they were accepted, but those remaining created a small area for themselves. Within a few short years the two "colonies" of New Holland had successfully blended together. Christians and non-Christians could live and work together in New Holland.

The Dutch colony comprised an area much larger than present day New York. It included land on both sides of the Hudson River, northward and southward. The Duke of York, in England, was given title to the new English colony. He in turn gave the land west of Hudson River to Lord Berkeley and Sir George Carteret.

In less than twenty years, the New York Colony grew and prospered to the point that in 1683 the New York Assembly was established to create laws for the colony. New York had been granted some independence in the form of self government.

In order to attract settlers to their colony, Lord Berkeley and Sir George Carteret offered free land, freedom of religion, and a democratic system of local government. The colony of New Jersey was begun. With the offer of free land and religious freedom, many Quakers came to this new colony.

The Quakers were a new religious group in England. They separated themselves from other English citizens by their clothing, the way they practiced their religion, and by their use of the English language. They used the pronouns "thee" and "thou," which made other Englishmen uncomfortable. But most of all, they practiced peace.

William Penn was a leader among the English Quakers, but his father was one of England's great military leaders. It was through the influence of his father that he and other Quakers were kept out of jail, though eventually he was jailed for a short period of time. Penn, having grown up in the influential portion of society, used his connections and influence to have the King grant him land and a charter for a colony. Again the King was able to use the new world as a dumping ground for dissenters.

In 1681, William Penn was given a charter for a colony. Pennsylvania was established. Following the Quaker philosophy, Penn created an atmosphere in which the Indians would hopefully be

Skull & Heap: *East Prospect of the City of Philadelphia (detail). The Library Company of Philadelphia.*

treated fairly and all people would be welcome. He also established a democratic system of local government, believing each man had a right to a say in the government.

☆☆

In the 1700's, if in debt and unable to pay, an Englishman could be convicted of a crime and sentenced to jail. In order to clear out the honest, but debt-ridden individuals in prison, the King ordered a new colony to be created.

In 1732, Georgia, the last of the North American English colonies, was begun. In an attempt to establish an ideal colony, liquor and slavery were banned from the beginning.

After a few short years, the colony was failing. Indians, hot wet weather, and difficulty clearing land made free Englishmen go to other colonies. Only a slave could be forced to do the hard, painful work of clearing the Georgia land, and so the King in England reversed himself and allowed the colony to be open to slavery. By the 1750's, Georgia was a growing, prospering colony.

The English colonies in the Americas stretched from the Caribbean Sea, north along the Atlantic coast to the top of North America.

The British Colonial System

☆☆☆☆☆☆☆☆☆☆☆☆☆☆☆☆☆☆☆☆☆☆☆☆☆

From the beginning of establishing the colonies, the government in England had to develop a plan or system for governing them. Since the distance between the ruling country and the colonies often required two or more months travel time to send a message from one to the other, the colonies were given some freedom to grow. In the beginning, they produced little for the mother country. They were a place for excess population to move and a place to dump the mother country's problem citizens. At their start, they provided little else for England.

Therefore it was decided to let each colony handle all its local matters. To do this, a governor was appointed by the King. This Royal Governor would then appoint local officials, who would execute local laws. The Governor could summon and dismiss colonial legislatures, having the right to veto colonial laws passed by the legislature. But the Governors were made dependent on their colonies for their salary, and so a mutual dependence developed between the colonial legislatures and the Royal Governors. So long as they held the purse strings, the Governors would listen to what the legislatures would have to say. They might disagree, but the Governors would always listen.

Many of the colonies created a two house legislature. The lower house was elected by the male citizens of the colony, while the upper house was appointed by the King or the Governor. The lower house handled the financial matters of the colony and the Governor's salary.

Along with democratic rule, a court system was developed in each colony. Not tied to the laws of England 3,000 miles away, the colonial juries decided cases based on what they felt was right, often not referring to English law.

Navigation Acts   By the mid 1600's, England had been moving in the direction of a strong internal system of commerce. It was believed that by forcing the colonies to trade only with the mother country, English industry would grow and prosper, which in turn would allow the colonies to grow and prosper. Previously, for nearly fifty years, England had passed a series of trade laws to stimulate internal commerce.

England patterned itself after the successful Dutch example. By the 1650's, the Dutch dominated world trade with over 10,000 trade ships at sea. The Dutch control monopolized the trade in the East and West Indies. To try to cut into the Dutch trade, in 1650, Parliament barred foreign ships from its colonies without special licenses. Ships were also prevented from delivering goods to England. England was cutting off the Dutch from their English business.

Parliament's actions caused three wars with the Dutch. The last one yielded New York to England in 1664.

By 1660, the English fleet had grown and enforcement of the trade laws was fairly common. Once the fleet was strong enough,

Parliament saw fit to pass the Navigation Act of 1660. It allowed only English ships to go to English colonies. The ships going to these ports must have crews which were at least 3/4 English. This included colonists who were English. The Navigation Act also said products such as sugar, tobacco, cotton, ginger, and dyes, could not be shipped from the colonies to any place other than within the English Empire. Parliament wanted to control world trade in these products.

In 1663, Parliament added to the first Navigation Act, declaring that any product which was being shipped to another English colony had to first pass through England. This gave England complete control in all colonial trade. Now the colonies became fully dependent on their mother country.

Board of Trade   By the late 1600's, the companies which had established many of the colonies were either unwilling or no longer able to handle their colonies, which had grown quickly, well beyond the expectations of most. In 1696, all the colonies which were not yet the personal property of the King were made his property, and the Board of Trade was created.

The Board of Trade became the ruling body for all the English colonies in North America and the Caribbean. They selected, with the King's approval, the man for the position of Colonial Governor and they also had the right to review all colonial laws passed. This, in theory, gave the Board the right to reject or accept any law passed by a colony. To be fair to the colonies, the King and Parliament had each colony send one representative to sit on the Board and express the opinions of that colony. It was hoped that the constant interaction between the Board and the representatives of the colonies would lead to a greater understanding between the two. By allowing the colonies to participate on the Board of Trade, the King hoped that their opinions and feelings would be expressed and taken into account before any decision would be made. Since they were represented on the Board, Parliament believed that the colonies would have no reason to complain about the decisions made.

Mercantilism   In the beginning of the 1700s, a nation's wealth was measured by its ability to supply all of its own needs. *Mercantilism* is the name for this economic theory and it dominated colonial rule. The Board of Trade was concerned with commerce in order to make England a self-sufficient nation.

The colonies provided the raw materials, such as wood, cotton, and other crops. These in turn led to the wealth of the mother country by which these items would be turned into saleable products. The colonists would then purchase products, which had been produced from their raw materials, from the mother country.

This system of internal commerce would stimulate trade between colonies and mother country. To encourage the purchase of products from within the nation, taxes would be placed on foreign products. This would cause the foreign products to be too expensive to purchase and would also prevent gold from leaving the English economy.

For the longest time, no one thought to challenge this theory since it seemed to work for the benefit of both the mother country, England, and its English colonies.

In 1696, with the Board of Trade now in charge, the Board enforced the Navigation Acts. As the eighteenth century began, the Board of Trade added to the list of products England wanted to control. Furs, rice, molasses, and copper were now restricted to England only.

The colonies were viewed as partners in the system and not as dependents of the system. The colonies benefited from the system since it allowed them to grow and develop as trading partners with the mother country. Both the mother country and the colonies grew wealthier.

The shipbuilding trades, which were unaffected by the laws, actually flourished in Massachusetts and Rhode Island. England needed ships. The craftsmen and wood in the colonies made it an ideal place for the ship building industry to grow. Many types of crafts developed and the craftsmen found strong markets for their products. Barrel making, shoemaking, and other skills thrived, as their products were sold around the world in other English colonies.

Early iron mills were encouraged in the colonies, but in 1750 new iron mills were prohibited. The English iron mills wanted the exclusive profits and trade from the iron production. For the first time, English merchants exercised control in trade in a manner which truly hurt the iron producing colonies. The colonies of Virginia, Maryland, New Jersey, and Pennsylvania were the most affected. Iron was plentiful in these colonies and the first resentment towards the Navigation Acts was felt.

The affected colonies did not listen to the new regulations. Even after the Navigation Act of 1750, new iron mills opened in Pennsylvania. By 1775, 1/7 of the world's iron came from the American colonies.

While the colonies flourished, a wealthy class of American colonists developed. They wanted to continue to accumulate property and wealth and they began to see the Navigation Acts as an obstacle. The foreign products they wished to purchase had to first pass through the hands of the English merchants, who then sold it to the colonists after first raising the prices of the items. When disagreements arose between the colonists and the English merchants, the Board of Trade seemed to always be on the side of the English merchant in the mother country. The colonists always lost. To avoid increased prices on foreign goods, smuggling became common practice in the colonies and was even considered respectable. Colonial disregard for the Navigation Acts grew. England did little about the problem.

Still, the colonies flourished in a system rigged against them, and England prospered as well. Wealth flowed into the nation as the mother country and her colonies experienced good times.

When they felt like it, the colonists ignored the Navigation Acts. Because of their close proximity to the French West Indies, American colonists smuggled in French wine and molasses. Sold cheaply, these products were easy for the colonists to obtain. The coastline was too great for the British Navy to completely watch. The taxes for many foreign products were almost never collected.

Though they may have disagreed with England at times, the colonists were still loyal Englishmen and they still tried to obey the laws. The colonial authorities had little power to force the colonists to obey because they never needed to force colonial obedience. Generally, the colonists willingly complied with the laws. Thus, though things were unbalanced in favor of the mother country, the system worked.

Early Colonial Wars and Their Effects

☆☆☆☆☆☆☆☆☆☆☆☆☆☆☆☆☆☆☆☆☆☆☆☆☆☆☆

In pursuit of the mercantile theory, England made many enemies. The other nations of Europe were also trying to establish control over trade and their colonies as well. With everyone attempting to control trade, conflicts between nations were bound to happen.

Conflicts between England and both the French and Spanish during the 16th, 17th and 18th centuries were almost constant. As far as the English were concerned, the Spanish ships sailing from the Americas and loaded with treasure, were fair game on the high seas. Among the English, becoming a privateer, a government approved pirate, was looked upon as a respectable profession. From the time of the first colonies in the new world, conflicts at sea were normal.

The waters of the North Atlantic and the shores off Canada provided more fish than anyone could hope to catch. But disagreements arose as to where the fishermen could put into port. The fishermen needed places to dry and salt their catch before returning to Europe. Once the fishing industry developed in the North Atlantic, the French and English were always fighting over places

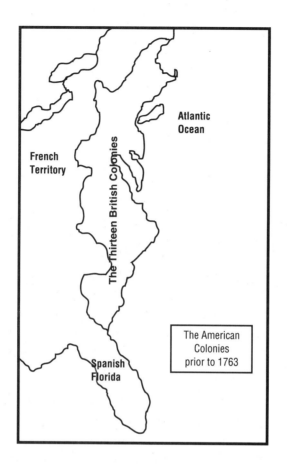

French Territory

Atlantic Ocean

The Thirteen British Colonies

Spanish Florida

The American Colonies prior to 1763

along the North American shores of Nova Scotia, Newfoundland, and Maine to salt their fish.

Not happy to fight among themselves, the European nations allied themselves with various Indian tribes and encouraged them to wage war against the other nations. The French dominated fur trade with the Indians and the English wanted it. The English allied themselves with the Iroquois Six Nations and with the tribes along the Mississippi River and Ohio Valley. They hoped that by backing treaties with the Indians they could eventually dominate the fur trade.

In the beginning the English colonies had little to do with the English wars. From 1689 to 1697, during King William's War, the colonies played only a small part in the conflict. They were too small and too weak to have much effect on the outcome and so they were largely ignored.

During Queen Anne's War, from 1702 to 1713, England fought both France and Spain at the same time. The war was mostly fought in Europe and England was victorious, forcing France to give up Nova Scotia, Newfoundland and the Hudson Bay areas in North America. The English foothold in America was growing and strengthening.

By the time of King George's War, 1740 to 1748, the conflicts raged worldwide. Wherever the warring nations had colonies, Asia, Africa, or the Americas, the fighting occurred. In 1744, King George's War expanded to include the American colonies.

The French instigated Indians raids on the English settlers. They provided arms, ammunition and even payment for each settler killed. To the colonial settlers, nothing was feared more than Indian raids, and the French were now behind the raids.

Now the colonies were more than willing to participate in the war. Many of the English colonies claimed areas in the Ohio Valley, but France claimed the entire area for itself and fought to keep out the English. France was trying to keep the extremely profitable fur trade to itself. Many in the colonies wanted a greater portion of the fur trade and were willing to take risks to secure it.

King George's War was not an English victory nor was it a loss in the Americas. The French were still able to hold onto the Ohio Territory to the west of the English colonies.

But a change occurred in the colonies because of the war. Because of the trade involved in supplying an army during a war, many of the colonists grew quite prosperous while supporting the army in the west; thus the colonies expanded farther into the disputed territories. Unlike previous conflicts, the colonies now felt the French and Indian threat more than ever.

In 1754, Benjamin Franklin of Pennsylvania proposed a loose union of the colonies and suggested a meeting of all the colonies to discuss the matter. Many of the colonies immediately rejected the idea of any type of union. They felt it threatened their independence and refused to attend any meeting wishing to remain separate from the other colonies.

But seven colonies sent representatives to attend the meeting in Albany, New York. Those delegates who attended this Albany Convention approved a plan for a common defense against the Indians. Yet the legislature of each colony whose delegate attended and approved of the plan rejected any idea of a union between the colonies. Franklin's Albany Plan was dead. However, changes in attitudes in the colonies were occurring, but very slowly. Cooperation between the different colonies was not yet ready to be achieved.

The single greatest difference between England and the American colonies was the social mobility. In England, tenant farmers would remain tenant farmers for life, always working for another man. In America, an individual who came across the Atlantic as a servant could finish his required seven years of service and start to build his own farm. Therefore, many came as indentured servants, someone who signed a contract to work for seven years to pay for his passage to America. In a single generation, a family went from servant to farm owner, or from poor farmer to large land owner. Poor farmers became wealthy plantation owners. The old rules of England did not apply in the colonies. A man could work hard and move up and become wealthy.

Even those who did not own land had a chance to improve themselves. Store clerks and workers studied to become prominent lawyers. Small tradesmen grew into wealthy businessmen. Many of the colonies required little for a man to participate in government and vote.

Still there was an aristocracy, or an upper social class, which developed in the colonies. But, unlike in England, one did not need a royal title or aristocratic birth. With hard work, one was able to enter into the elite upper social class.

A new attitude was developing in the American colonies. The opportunity for growth and wealth, along with the social and physical mobility of the people, caused the colonists to demanded a more responsive government. With what seemed like unlimited land available, the English colonists were always on the move west. They expected their government to move with them and help them as they needed it. The colonists were experiencing a prosperity unseen before and they expected it to continue.

Unfortunately, this was about to change.

The French and Indian War King George's War showed the French that they needed to secure their lands in America. After the war, the French established a string of forts beginning in present day Michigan heading southward. They hoped this action would protect them against any English intrusion, while increasing their contact and friendship with the Indians.

Although neither side was able to lay claim to victory, King George's War had one result the French hated. During the war, English soldiers and colonists went into the Ohio Valley to fight the French. Although engaged in warfare, the English built their own string of forts as protection and as supply depots. When the war ended, many of the colonists remained in the west and began fur trapping. It was just a matter of time before the two nations would be at war again.

During the next few years, the Virginia colony sent settlers and trappers into the Ohio Valley. In 1752, the French attacked one of the Virginia outposts and drove the traders, trappers, and settlers back into Pennsylvania.

The Virginia colony decided to send a small armed party into the Ohio territory it claimed. Its purpose was to tell the French that they were trespassing on English land. To do this, Virginia sent a young surveyor who was also an officer in the Virginia militia, George Washington.

It was not difficult for Washington to make contact with the French, who told him that they were taking the entire Ohio Valley for France. Washington returned to Williamsburg, the colonial capital of Virginia, with the French demand to withdraw from the valley.

The Virginia Governor decided military action was going to be needed. Washington was promoted to Lieutenant Colonel in the Virginia militia and returned to the Ohio Valley with 150 men to seize an important junction point of French forts.

Washington was led to believe that the French position was weak. Instead, it was well armed and firmly in French possession, with strong support from the local Indian tribes. Washington and his men were surrounded by the French and their Indian allies. After a short battle in which the Virginians were badly beaten, Washington was tricked into signing a surrender.

The document was written entirely in French and Washington could not read French. He was not told that the document said Virginia surrendered its claims in the Ohio Valley. He believed he was agreeing to return to Virginia and that he and his army would not fight again. Washington was then sent back home to Virginia with what remained of his army.

George Washington *As a colonial leader of Virginia with military experience, the Second Continental Congress in Philadelphia selected George Washington as the man to lead the colonial army. Library of Congress*

Although Washington surrendered, Virginia looked at him as a hero. He had been able to strike a blow against the French in the Ohio Valley. The French and Indian War had begun.

In 1755, General Braddock of the regular British army led a force of 1,500 men against the French. The army consisted of mostly regular British soldiers and only a few hundred colonial militia. Looked down upon by the British officers for being a colonial militia officer, George Washington was reduced in rank and assigned as an aide to Braddock during Braddock's attack of the French.

General Braddock refused to listen to Washington or his knowledge of the French strength and his experience fighting the Indians. Instead, Braddock marched his army into the wilderness, pulling artillery through the woods where there were no trails. The advance was very slow and noisy. When they finally penetrated the Ohio Valley, the French and Indians were waiting. Decisively defeated, Braddock was killed while Washington was able to escape with barely 500 men.

The regular British army tried to blame the colonial militia and their leader, Washington, for the defeat. But it was quickly proven to be the fault of General Braddock. Washington quickly learned how the British army worked and thought. The Royal Governor of Virginia promoted Washington back to colonel.

Many of the Indian tribes were not aligned with either side and both the French and English tried to win them over. It was common for both sides to try to hire the Indians for a specific battle or for the entire war. The British offered five pounds (about 12 dollars in today's currency) for each scalp the Indians brought back as proof of killing. The French offered 200 pounds (about 500 dollars in today's currency). Most of the Indian nations fought with the French.

The Indians attacked with vengence, often going after unarmed settlements and killing not only the men, but the women and children as well. The settlers along the western frontier feared these Indian attacks and hated the French for instigating them.

By 1756 the war had spread to Europe. The English wanted to win this war at any cost. They saw an opportunity to rid the North American continent of the French and they needed it to happen. To accomplish this, the English government spent more than it could afford. They built up the navy, while also sending large armies to fight in North America.

In the beginning the British and the colonial armies suffered many defeats at the hands of the French. The Prime Minister of England, William Pitt, promoted General Wolfe and placed him in charge of the North American fighting. Quickly defeats turned to victories.

By the next winter, Fort Duquesne fell, then Fort Niagara, and finally Quebec. The British had clearly become the dominant army in North America. In the battle for Quebec, the two leading Generals, Wolfe and Montcalm, both died during the fighting. But it was too late for the French. In 1760, the French lost Montreal and abandoned Canada to the British. The French sugar islands in West Indies also fell to the British. By the end of that year, it was apparent that the war was over and that the French had been defeated.

In the Treaty of Paris of 1763, the French abandoned all claims in North America, giving all their lands and territories east of the Mississippi River over to the British. Only the islands in the Caribbean were returned to France.

The British now owned half the continent.

Since most of the Indian tribes that had become involved fought with the French, the British wanted to hurt them after the war. The British Commander in the west, Lord Jeffrey Amherst, suggested infecting tribes with smallpox to kill and weaken them. Once weakened, he wanted to hunt down the survivors. Amherst's plan was rejected, not because it was inhumane or cruel, but from fear that the smallpox might infect some of the English colonists. The war with the French ended, but many of the Indian tribes fought on. Chief Pontiac tried to drive out the British in the Ohio Valley and failed. It became apparent that continued fighting with the Indians was too costly and mostly ineffective.

Another solution had to be tried.

Problems Begin Between the Colonies and England

☆☆☆☆☆☆☆☆☆☆☆☆☆☆☆☆☆☆☆☆☆☆☆☆☆

To quiet things down along the frontier, the British proposed the Proclamation of 1763. They agreed to the Indian demand that no new settlements be established in the west and that the British restrict travel across the Appalachian Mountains. The British now required traders to have a license to trade with Indians and required additional permits to cross to the west.

Since protection from the Indians on the western frontier was almost nonexistent and would be too expensive to try to establish, and since there seemed to be enough land in the east, the British government agreed to outlaw settlements west of the Appalachian Mountains.

For many of the colonists, the territories to the west were the only lands they could afford in order to begin their own farms. One just had to go west to take free land. For these colonists, the halting of westward expansion was unthinkable. Many looked on this agreement as ridiculous and ignored the treaty. In a few short years, frontiersmen like Daniel Boone were to be crossing the Cumberland Gap leading settlers west.

Many of the colonists were angry about the British Proclamation of 1763. Settlements in the west were to be abandoned or if the settlers chose to remain in the Indian territories, they would be left on their own. This was unacceptable to the colonists. To appease them, the British claimed that the Proclamation of 1763 was to be temporary. By 1764, most of the Indian tribes accepted the peace terms of the British and peace was achieved in the west.

Even with the restrictions of westward expansion, the colonists rejoiced at the British victory over France. They expected good times to return to the colonies.

After the war ended, many British soldiers remained in the colonies. The officers and men of the regular British army looked down on their American brothers, referring to them as "innkeepers with guns." Resentment between the two began immediately.

During the war, the colonists were happy to let the British regulars fight for them and protect them; now they wanted the soldiers gone from the American shores. The British government was not ready to remove them so quickly. Relations between the English government and the colonies began to weaken.

Even before conflicts between the colonists and the British developed, the colonists began to experience their own internal problems. During the French and Indian War, in Massachusetts, Samuel Adams and some friends started a newspaper, "The Independent Advertiser." In it, the Royal Governor of Massachusetts was attacked on issues of the day. The newspaper lasted only a short time, but it became accepted in Massachusetts that a challenge to government authority was reasonable. Sam Adams and his friends began to develop a small following people who were willing to openly challenge the government when they felt the government was wrong.

Challenges to government authority became more common and acceptable as the war ended. Often it was a conflict between eastern and western portions of a colony. In Pennsylvania, after the Proclamation of 1763, a small uprising of settlers from the west occurred. The western settlers wanted protection from the Indians and demanded money for a militia to help defend the western settlements. The British regular troops refused to help them; after all, the colonists had been ordered to abandon their western settlements.

A group of settlers from the west, known as "The Paxton Boys," after having been outvoted in the Pennsylvania legislature for money for a militia, took it upon themselves to attack the Indians they felt threatening them. The Paxton Boys then marched on the colonial capitol. Furious after fighting the Indians on their own, the Paxton Boys were unpredictable. Benjamin Franklin was able to calm them down by promising them bounties for each of the Indian scalps they took. Things along the western frontier were beginning to heat up. The English settlers and the Indians were not getting along too well. Tensions grew.

☆☆

During the French and Indian War, Parliament took control of colonial courts and allowed officials to search colonists' homes for smuggled goods without obtaining warrants from a court. Many of the colonists were willing to accept these actions as emergency measures during a war. But now the war was over and Parliament was continuing the practices and in some cases expanding them.

James Otis in Boston argued against this practice in the Massachusetts legislature, saying that Parliament's actions were violating their rights as Englishmen.

Patrick Henry was an attorney handling a case against the Church of England in the colony of Virginia. In Virginia, as in most of the colonies, the church was an official part of the government.

Henry attacked ministers of the Anglican Church, saying they took money from the colonists for their own use. For the first time, the King, the Church of England, and the colonial system were openly challenged in court.

In 1763, Henry declared in court that King George III had misruled his people by allowing this practice to continue. He went further, saying that since the King allowed these acts to continue, he was no longer the father of his people. Henry stated that the King and his subjects had a contract with each other and if either side violated this trust, the contract would no longer be valid. Some people in the court yelled treason, others agreed with Henry.

At the same time that Patrick Henry was in court making statements against the King, and the "Paxton Boys" from Pennsylvania took it upon themselves to decide English policy on the frontier, Parliament now began reviewing laws passed by the colonial legislature in Virginia. Even though it may have always been allowed, the British government had never before used its privilege to check over colonial laws. For the first time, Britain reviewed and then disallowed laws passed by the Virginia House of Burgesses.

With colonial leaders speaking out against the King, with colonists taking action on their own and trying to set frontier policy, and with Parliament disallowing colonial laws, by the end of 1763, the mood in the colonies was changing.

The colonists saw that by challenging the government or even by taking action on their own, they got the results they wanted. It was a lesson they learned quickly.

The British Debt   When the French and Indian War ended, the British national debt had doubled. In addition to the burden of a huge debt, the English nation faced the cost of administrating the enlarged empire as well. Parliament felt it was too much for the

King George III *King George III was the British ruler during the American Revolution. Often guided by bad advice from his ministers, King George added to the bad feelings between the colonist and England. Library of Congress*

British taxpayer to handle alone. The cost to maintain the American colonies had risen from 70,000 pounds a year before the French and Indian War to over 350,000 pounds per year after the war. It would be necessary to raise additional money.

Most of the British citizens in England looked down on the American colonists. In England, the colonists were viewed as being barely civilized, ignorant, and crude. Anger existed in Britain towards them because during the recent war, many colonists still traded with the French in the West Indies for sugar, molasses, and rum. It was felt that they had betrayed their country in war.

With huge debts facing Britain and the American colonies growing increasingly wealthier, Parliament decided to take a more active role in governing the colonies. The freedom the colonists had experienced for 100 years was about to change.

George Grenville was a financial expert in England and was appointed Prime Minister in 1763. He was less concerned about rights than he was about paying off England's debt. Under the guidance of Prime Minister Grenville, Parliament, for the first time, tried to raise money in the colonies.

The Sugar Act To help pay off the national debt and raise money to maintain the expanded American empire, Prime Minister Grenville proposed the Sugar Act of 1764. This law placed taxes on sugar, coffee, wines, and other products imported into the colonies. Foreign products, which were imported through Britain to the American colonies, had their taxes doubled. However, the tax on foreign molasses was cut in half. Since molasses was smuggled into the colonies most of the time, Parliament hoped that reducing the tax would make smuggling less profitable and help to end the practice. Since almost none of the taxes due on molasses was being collected, Parliament hoped that at least some of the reduced tax on molasses would be collected. Finally, the Sugar Act ended the practice which allowed a colony to print a limited amount of money, on its own, to help its economy grow. England was now going to closely administer its American colonies.

This was the first law since the Navigation Acts to raise money in the American colonies. Even the Navigation Acts were very minor, being used only to help regulate commerce. Now Parliament was not trying to help commerce; the sole purpose of the Sugar Act was to raise money for the government.

No one in Parliament expected the reaction the Sugar Act received. Americans refused to accept the idea that Parliament could tax them. James Otis in his pamphlet, **"The Rights of the British Colonies Asserted and Proved,"** said that every man should be free from taxes that either he or his representative did not consent to. The New York Assembly said, "Who can call that his own which can be taken away at the pleasure of another?" New York felt Parliament was taking money away from colonists without the right to do so.

To the members of Parliament, it didn't seem necessary to ask the colonies for permission. No one was asked when taxes were passed for other English colonies, and no other nation asked its colonies for permission. The colonies existed for the benefit of the mother country. This is the way it had always been and would always be as far as Parliament could see.

The King in London said that Parliament had the good of the entire empire at heart and besides, most British citizens in England also had no say in the selection of the members of Parliament and therefore no say in the laws passed for them.

This idea may have made sense in London, but the American colonists were used to electing their own legislatures. As to the previous taxes of the Navigation Acts, the colonists had been cheating on these laws for years. As far the colonists were concerned, these laws barely existed. They had smuggled in the products they wanted and generally did as they pleased for nearly 100 years. Now they were being told to join the Empire.

Sam Adams was asked by the Boston legislature to write a response to the Sugar Act. He said, *"If you let Parliament tax your trade, why not next your land? why not your produce?"* He put the protest against the Sugar Act into clear wording for the average colonist to understand. Parliament had no right to tax the colonies without their consent, resulting in the slogan "*No Taxation Without Representation.*" Writings of Otis and Adams were circulated to the other colonies.

The level of protest raised throughout the colonies surprised everyone. Threats were made against the lives of the British tax collectors. Many became too frightened to try to do anything other than sit by and wait.

The House of Burgesses, the colonial legislature of Virginia, met in Williamsburg. At first some felt that to question the authority of Parliament and the King was treason. But after months of debate and argument, in early 1765, the House of Burgesses agreed upon a letter to be sent to the King. It was a plea to protect the traditional rights of Virginians and to allow them to continue to conduct their own government business and taxation.

Virginians only elected representatives to the House of Burgesses and not Parliament. The letter echoed the cry which was being heard throughout the colonies, "NO TAXATION WITHOUT REPRESENTATION."

In May of 1765, the House of Burgesses agreed upon a series of resolutions to be included in their letter to the King, declaring:

1 The colonists had rights as Englishmen and the Virginia legislature felt their rights were not being observed;

2 Taxation could only be passed by the people or by those chosen by the people, and since they did not elect the members of Parliament, Parliament had no right to pass taxes for them;

3 Only those selected by the people had the right to choose how to tax;

4 The King had always accepted these principles and therefore must continue to treat colonies in the manner which they had been handled for 100 years;

5 Therefore, only the General Assembly of the colony had a right to tax that colony; that to do otherwise was to destroy British and American freedom.

As a colonial representative to the government in England, Benjamin Franklin suggested a compromise to end the disagreement. Franklin wanted Parliament to tell the colonies how much their share of the debt would be and allow them to decide how they would pay for it. He had no authority to promise anything for the separate colonies but believed that he could help convince them that they must accept their share of the debt.

Parliament viewed things a little differently. The abundant resources and simple life of the colonies, along with the fact that England had allowed them to develop at their own pace, caused them to grow and prosper. Now they were needed to become part of the community of England and assume their responsibilities. For Parliament, this meant payment of taxes.

Even before Virginia's letter of protest reached the shores of England, Grenville went to Parliament to create a new set of taxes to replace the Sugar Act. The members of Parliament did not understand why the colonies were protesting. They believed it was the items which were being taxed which caused the problems, not the taxes themselves.

Stamp Act In 1765, Parliament decided on a different course of action. It would raise money by taxing newspapers, legal documents, and licenses. This is the way taxes were collected in England and surely the colonies could not object to being treated just like other Englishmen. Parliament collected over 100,000 pounds annually in England and hoped to collect 60,000 pounds annually in the American colonies to help pay the costs of defending and protecting the colonies. Unlike the Sugar Act, the Stamp Tax was a direct tax on the colonists themselves and not on products imported. Parliament believed this to be fair, since the larger colonies where more business was transacted would have to pay more.

But not everyone in Parliament agreed. One voice raised in protest to the taxes was Colonel Barre, who had fought in the colonies during the French and Indian War. He said that the attitude of English officials "caused the blood of those sons of liberty to recoil within them." When Colonial Barre's speech of protest was reported to the colonies, they were proud to be referred to as the "Sons of Liberty."

In Massachusetts, Samuel Adams and his friends established a group to protest what they felt were English injustices toward the colonies. Taking the lead provided for them in Colonel Barre's speech, Adams called the group the "Sons of Liberty." Having led protests before against the Governor of Massachusetts, Adams seemed the logical choice to head this new protest group.

When the first stamps arrived in New York harbor for distribution to all the colonies, all the ships in the harbor lowered their flags in protest. As the stamps arrived in the different colonies, some of the stamps were seized and burned by mobs. When they could, the British officials locked up the stamps for safety.

During the summer of 1765, the Sons of Liberty were using violence in their protests against the tax. With Sam Adams at their head, they marched to the home of Boston's tax collector and looted the house. The next night, the home of Lieutenant Governor Thomas Hutchinson was also destroyed. Ransacking and burning Hutchinson's house, the Sons of Liberty destroyed government

The Stamp Act   During the uproar over the Stamp Act, colonists in many port cities marched in protest against the new tax. Library of Congress

records concerning taxes and tax collection. Sam Adams and his followers were blamed for instigating the riot. It was clearly a protest that had gotten out of hand. Adams, in his newspaper, blamed strangers from out of town for the second night of rioting and a wild mob for the first.

In Virginia, Patrick Henry led the debate in the House of Burgesses, vowing that only the House had the right to tax Virginians.

Faster than Sam Adams could have imagined, Sons of Liberty groups appeared throughout the colonies. These groups prevented the taxes from being collected. In Maryland, the Stamp Tax collector had to run to New York to hide for safety. But that did not help, because a Sons of Liberty group in New York tracked him down and forced him to resign his post. Most other Stamp Tax collectors met a similar fate as they were forced to flee and resign their positions. The mood of protest swept across the American colonies.

In June, the Massachusetts colony called for a Stamp Act Congress. Each colony was to meet in October to discuss the Stamp Act and the problems it caused. Meeting in New York, the Stamp Act Congress passed a series of resolutions of protest, declaring Parliament had no right to interfere with the colonies. They went further than just the Stamp Act, saying Parliament had no authority to tax or eliminate trial by jury as it had done in some colonies.

The men who met in New York were some of the leading citizens of each colony. Timothy Ruggles and James Otis represented Massachusetts, Robert Livingston came from New York, John Rutledge from South Carolina, and Edward Tilghman and Caesar Rodney of Maryland. Together, these leading spokesmen from the colonies put forth a new idea, declaring that the colonists should think of themselves as Americans, not as Virginians or New Yorkers. It was a new concept, one which would take ten years to grow and flourish.

By November 1, 1765, when the Stamp Act was to have gone into effect, Americans boycotted anything which would require a stamp as the Stamp Act Congress suggested. Slowly the boycott grew stronger. Stamp Tax officials were helpless to take any action. Between the boycott and the violent protests, the Stamp Act became a dead issue and no taxes were collected. Colonial action had succeeded.

Parliament was again surprised at the amount of protest the Stamp Act generated. They expected some protesting, which is normal whenever any kind of tax is passed by any government, but not the extreme anger which occurred. In part, the force of the protests happened because of whom the taxes most hurt. The Stamp Act placed taxes on newspapers, legal documents, birth certificates, affecting merchants and tradesmen and anyone who dealt with papers. The people who would have to pay the most were often the leaders and among the most outspoken and articulate persons of the colonies. Causing these people to become angry was a bad move by Parliament.

As 1765 closed, Sam Adams and his younger cousin, John Adams, were asked to write a protest against the Stamp Act by the legislature in Massachusetts. Sam's fire and John's knowledge of the law led to a good union between the cousins and a long political relationship. On December 17, 1765 the Boston Customs House reopened, allowing all ships to enter or leave the harbor without the need of stamps on legal documents. The Sons of Liberty, across the many colonies, celebrated.

The Sons of Liberty had become the protectors of American liberties. A new sense of freedom swept over the colonies. Their successful boycotts and protests showed Parliament that the colonies knew their rights and were willing to fight for them.

When Parliament removed the Stamp Act, it felt it necessary to pass the Declaratory Act. The Declaratory Act said that Parliament always had the right to tax colonies. It expressed the idea that the colonies were subordinate to Parliament and Parliament could pass any law it wished to "bind the colonies and people of America." The colonies may have won this small battle, but Parliament wanted them know who was in charge. Parliament was preparing for the next fight.

During the uproar over the Stamp Tax, Parliament saw fit to pass a special law for the New York colony. It was told to provide additional money to be used by the British army for certain supplies which Parliament specified. Since no other colony was asked to spend this "additional money" and since the government in England paid for these provisions for soldiers in Europe, the New York colony refused to pay. Things between the colonies and the British government were beginning to fall apart. What had been a good working relationship for over 100 years was changing.

Battle lines between the Parliament and the colonies were being drawn.

Parliament Raises the Level of Conflict

☆☆☆☆☆☆☆☆☆☆☆☆☆☆☆☆☆☆☆☆☆☆☆☆☆

Quartering Act If Parliament was trying to settle its differences with the American colonies, it was going about it in the wrong manner. Even before the last protest against the Stamp Act had occurred, Parliament saw fit to pass the Quartering Act. This law required the colonists to house and feed new British troops who were being sent to the colonies. Suddenly the colonists were being forced to have soldiers live in their homes. This only occurred in a few of the colonies, but the leaders of all the colonies feared that this was the beginning of an English conspiracy to take away their rights as Englishmen.

Why were the soldiers in the colonies and whom were they there to fight? The colonists became concerned. Did Parliament believe that the colonists were the enemy? Some colonists were beginning to see Parliament as the enemy.

Once the Stamp Act had been removed as law, the colonists and England settled into an uneasy peace. Convinced that the housing of soldiers in people's homes would be temporary, many of the protest leaders began to ignore the situation. After all, they were told that the soldiers were being sent to protect the colonies from Indian attacks, not to enforce Parliament's laws.

Townshend Acts   The quiet peace between the colonies and Parliament was short lived. In June 1767, Parliament passed a series of taxes for the American colonies called the "Townshend Acts." Proposed by Lord Townshend, these laws placed taxes on glass, lead, paints, paper, and tea imported to the colonies.

The Acts also included a special provision suspending or prohibiting meetings of the New York legislature for not spending the additional money for the British soldiers to buy salt, vinegar, cider, or beer. Could Parliament suspend a colonial legislature? Word of these new taxes reached the colonies in the early part of 1768.

The questions of suspension of the legislature and of new taxes dominated all discussions in the colonies. If the New York legislature could be suspended, what real power did the colonial legislatures have? Who would be next?

John Dickinson of Pennsylvania wrote a simple pamphlet which gained wide distribution in the colonies. His "Letters from a farmer in Pennsylvania to the Inhabitants of the British Colonies" said Parliament is sovereign, but has no right to tax the colonies. Sam Adams went a step further, saying Parliament had no right to legislate for the colonies on any matter.

On February 4, 1768, the Massachusetts legislature approved Sam Adams' letter to be sent to the other colonies, saying that Parliament didn't even have the right to pass external taxes on the colonies if their purpose was only to raise money for the salaries of government officials in the colonies. This provision had the effect of making those in power dependent on Parliament and not on the colony where they lived, thus weakening the colonial legislatures to

Samuel Adams *Samuel Adams is often called the father of the American Revolution. He is considered the first to have advocated independence. In Boston, Adams began the Committees of Correspondence, and the Sons of Liberty. He was also one of the colonial leaders at the Boston Tea party and a member of the Second Continental Congress. Library of Congress*

the point where they could be completely ignored by the Governor. Together, the writings of Dickinson and Adams were discussed throughout the colonies.

When news of the distribution of the Massachusetts letter reached Parliament, it ordered the Governor of Massachusetts to dissolve the legislature. Under the direction of Parliament, Massachusetts lost its right to a legislature.

Parliament also sent two regiments of soldiers to Boston. Now the soldiers were being used to enforce the laws of Parliament, and Boston became a city occupied by an army. British patrols roamed the streets, as citizens became angrier. There was no enemy around. Were the citizens of Boston now considered to be the enemy by Parliament?

Things moved quickly in London since Prime Minister Townshend had died and was replaced by Lord North. He immediately had the Townsend Acts and all previous taxes removed. But the troops sent to Boston still arrived in September 1768. Boston remained occupied by the military and on October 1, 1768, the troops paraded through Boston. By November more troops arrived from England. Public demonstrations decreased, but tensions increased. This attempt to keep in check the Boston radicals appeared to work for the moment. The radicals were those who wanted a drastic change in the colonies. For them, nothing less then a complete change in colonial policy would do.

In the Virginia colony, 1769 opened calmly as the House of Burgesses returned to Williamsburg in April. As they gathered and discussed the recent taxes which Parliament passed for the colonies, extreme unrest caused by opposition to the taxes led the Royal Governor, Botetcourt, to disband the House of Burgesses. Word of the repeal of the taxes had not yet reached the colonies. The legislature was told to go home, since they would no longer be allowed to represent the citizens of Virginia. Virginia now had to face its own problem. Could the Royal Governor suspend a duly elected legislature of the people?

Immediately, the former members of the House met on their own and formed a committee to deal with the new problem. First, Governor Botetcourt removed the legislature. Could he next take away their liberties?

George Washington, a member of the disbanded House of Burgesses, presented a plan to the former members of the House. They declared that no item with a tax on it was to be imported into Virginia. This way they would not pay any tax and show Parliament that they were serious. They also hoped that this would scare the British merchants, who in turn, would be forced to go to Parliament and demand that it reverse its decision and remove the taxes. More than three fourths of the members of the disbanded House of Burgesses signed this new document.

The people of Virginia were now taking part in the protests against the way England was trying to rule the American colonies. The Virginia legislature had been forced to make a decision. Now they would stand with other colonies to the north in the protest against unfair British rule.

Virginia's boycott started out successfully and by the end of 1769, imports of these products into the colonies were cut in half. The colonists did not do without the taxed products; they just resorted to widespread smuggling.

Parliament chose to immediately deal with the problem of smuggling. They established courts to find and convict those cheating the system. These courts were set up without juries; in the cases brought before the court, a judge was to make the final decision. As payment for his time, the judge kept 1/3 of seized property. Corrupt officials saw an opportunity to gain quick wealth. Soon the courts went after law abiding merchants and shippers and seized their property. It was an easy way to steal money. Colonial anger went beyond anything Parliament had ever seen before.

The Governor of Virginia called for new elections for the House of Burgesses. He hoped for a change in the House of Burgesses. Unfortunately for the Governor he got what he wanted. Most of the former members were reelected, only now they had changed and become more radical than before. By his own action of disbanding the House of Burgesses, the Governor had made the House more radical and antagonistic. The Virginia legislative body drafted a letter to the King and Parliament, declaring, "No power on earth has a right to impose taxes upon a people without their consent."

Within a year the Virginia boycott weakened and was abandoned. The colonists still cared about these issues, but they were more concerned with day-to-day living. Parliament was now wise enough to let things settle quietly down. It was during this time period that the Committees of Correspondence were established by Sam Adams. The Committees, as they were called, were used to keep the lines of communication open between colonies. News events and topics for discussion were sent from colony to colony. Leaders in the separate colonies were now beginning to work together to handle common problems. Adams also used this quiet time to enhance his position in the colonies. He was building a radical alliance in each colony.

The First Shots Are Fired

☆☆☆☆☆☆☆☆☆☆☆☆☆☆☆☆☆☆☆☆☆☆☆

The Boston Massacre   Parliament had created a dangerous situation. The British soldiers were trained to fight wars, not to function as policemen. It was just a matter of time before angry citizens came into deadly conflict with the soldiers.

By late winter of 1770, the citizens of Boston were having many small arguments with the British soldiers. They resented the fact that many were unwelcomed guests in their homes. Were these soldiers just quartered there or were they spies for Parliament? The radical faction in Boston kept this question alive in the minds of the colonists.

On March 5, 1770, a group of Boston citizens began taunting and teasing a small unit of soldiers who were on duty. Tired of seeing British soldiers patrolling their streets when there was no enemy in sight, some Bostonians began throwing snowballs, and then sticks and stones at the soldiers.

Captain Thomas Preston, in charge of seven British soldiers, tried desperately to keep control of the situation. After they were hit by snowballs and sticks, he ordered his men to ignore the taunts and pull back from the colonists. The crowd grew larger and more daring as they began to throw stones. Next he ordered the crowd to disperse and go home. When this failed, Preston ordered one shot to be fired over the heads of the crowd.

The crowd pulled back in fear and some went home. Others remained. Those remaining again grew braver as they moved closer to the soldiers on duty. The verbal attacks became a constant roar as rocks, snowballs, and sticks seemed to come at the soldiers from everywhere. When they felt that the crowd was about to rush at them, in panic a few of the soldiers fired into the crowd.

The first man killed was Crispus Attucks. He was a mulatto, a mix of different races. His size and reputation among the dock workers had made him a leader of some of the men. A runaway slave, he was now a sailor. The crowd drew nearer to the British soldiers, hoping if they got close the British wouldn't be able to fire. The opposite occurred. Drawing even closer frightened the soldiers and they fired again into the crowd. Now five lay dead. This time the crowd fled home and for the moment, the incident was over.

Though a terrible spectacle, Sam Adams made the most of it. Declaring it to be a "massacre," Adams used his Committees of Correspondence to spread the word of the incident across the colonies. Playing it up as though it was a British assault on the unarmed harmless citizens of Boston, Adams raised the anger of colonists. His desire to force a wedge between the colonies and mother England was given strength.

Immediately after the "massacre," Sam Adams and John Hancock went to Governor Hutchinson to have the troops removed from Boston. John Hancock was a leading merchant and radical in Boston. To the Governor and British navy, Hancock was known to be one of the largest smugglers in New England. Adams and Hancock argued their point of view before the Governor and his council. Hutchinson refused to remove the troops. He had never

The Boston Massacre *Colonial wood engravings depicted British soldiers aiming and firing into defenseless colonists. It no longer mattered if this was the true story; many of the colonists believed it was true. Library of Congress*

forgotten how, when he was Lieutenant Governor, his home was attacked and burned by a mob led by Adams and his Sons of Liberty.

A town meeting was held in Boston, and everyone who attended agreed they wanted the soldiers removed from Boston. This time, all the leading citizens, including those known not to be among the radicals, pressured Governor Hutchinson to remove the soldiers. As they presented their case, even the Governor's personal council agreed removing the soldiers would prevent more violence. Hutchinson finally recanted and gave the order to send them out of Boston.

But even as the soldiers were preparing to leave Boston, the murder trial of the soldiers was about to begin. The Boston Massacre, as it was now called, had been a publicity dream for Sam Adams. This was about to change.

John Adams, Sam's cousin, was an attorney in Boston. Not as radical as his cousin at this time, John believed in the law above all else. Captain Preston came to John Adams asking him to defend him and the other soldiers. He believed he could probably never get a fair trial in Boston and that John Adams was his only hope. If Sam Adams' own cousin defended the soldiers, the people of Boston would have to listen to their side. John Adams agreed to defend them.

As the trial began, Sam Adams and the Sons of Liberty made the most out of the five deaths. They held a huge public funeral and marched the coffins through the streets of Boston. It was decided that Captain Preston was to be tried separately; the other soldiers would be tried together.

At Preston's trial, the prosecution, trying to show his guilt, was unable to get agreement on whether Preston ordered his troops to fire. Many said yes, while others said no. Then three slaves, who saw the entire incident, testified he did not give the order. They clearly heard the cry "fire" from off to the side. The jury found Captain Preston innocent.

In the soldiers trial, Adams used one of the wounded victims as the defense. Adams had Patrick Carr on the witness stand, asking him if he thought the soldiers were going to be hurt. Carr said yes and that the crowd yelled "Kill the soldiers." He finally admitted that the shooting was really self-defense by the soldiers. Testimony like Carr's helped Adams in his case. Five of the soldiers were found not guilty. Two were found guilty of manslaughter, which was a lesser crime. The jury said these two men fired when they really did not have to fire. But even with the guilty sentence, their punishment by the jury was slight. They had the thumbs on their right hands branded to show that they had been found guilty and then they were sent back to England.

With most of the soldiers found not guilty and minor punishments given to those convicted, the city of Boston and their Governor Hutchinson were not on good terms. Governor Hutchinson wanted to punish the citizens of Boston by teaching them a lesson. Having the legislature meet in a town meant prestige and financial advantages for that town. Hutchinson moved the legislature out of Boston to Cambridge. Many of the citizens of Boston became outraged by this insult from the Governor. Among those angered by the decision was the newly elected member of the legislature, John Adams.

The radicals decided not to abandon John Adams for defending Preston and the others. Hutchinson decided to try to split the radical leaders against each other and try to win some of the more moderate men to his side. In a move to win Hancock to his side, the Governor made him a colonel in the militia. Hutchinson hoped that by giving Hancock a position of power and prestige as well as additional income, it would put Hancock in his debt. Hutchinson was becoming desperate to try anything.

John Adams, writing under a different name, began a series of newspaper articles attacking the Governor and his actions. Adams declared the Governor anti-colonial and anti-Boston. John Adams now wrote in favor of the victims of the Boston Massacre, blaming their deaths on the insensitivity of the Governor and saying that if Hutchinson had removed the soldiers from Boston as requested earlier, the deaths would have been avoided.

In a strange twist of circumstance, some of Governor Hutchinson's letters written to a friend in England were obtained by Benjamin Franklin in London. These letters showed the Governor had a strong dislike for the colonists and condemned them. Franklin promised not to have the letters publicly printed. He hoped that by sending the letters to Boston, the patriots there would secretly use them to force Hutchinson to resign.

However, once in the hands of the radicals, the contents of the letters were made public. Embarrassed by what the letters contained, eventually Hutchinson was removed by Parliament. But that was not to be before he caused greater anger among the colonists of Massachusetts.

Tensions Rise to the Boiling Point

☆☆☆☆☆☆☆☆☆☆☆☆☆☆☆☆☆☆☆☆☆☆☆

In order to limit smuggling, the British sent a navy vessel, the *Gaspee*, to patrol the shores of New England. The *Gaspee* stayed off the shores of Newport, Rhode Island. The colonists in Rhode Island protested its presence, but the Commander of the *Gaspee* could care less about the protests and proceeded to follow his orders.

Early in 1772, while attempting to stop a ship suspected of smuggling, the *Gaspee* ran aground. It had followed the suspected ship into an inlet and became stuck in the mud. The captain of the escaping ship spread the news of the *Gaspee's* situation.

When several townspeople went on boats to approach the ship, the captain of the *Gaspee* ordered them away. A shot was fired from a boat, killing the captain. The colonists were now free to board the *Gaspee* without further incident.

The colonists who boarded the British naval vessel ordered the sailors to gather their belongings and depart. The colonists then set the ship afire, burning it down to its water line.

The Gaspee Incident *Colonists from Rhode Island attack and set afire the British Schooner, The* Gaspee, *but only after killing its captain. Library of Congress*

Secrecy was needed for the men who did this since if caught, they all would have been shot for their actions. Even though it became common knowledge, the colonists refused to testify against those who committed this criminal act. Parliament now believed that the colonists were totally lawless.

As 1772 drew to its end, the Governor of Massachusetts, Thomas Hutchinson, announced that from then on he would receive his salary from England and no longer from the Massachusetts legislature. The legislature now lost its little remaining power over the Governor. He was under the direct control of Parliament.

The situation in Boston was becoming worse. Tensions were on the rise. What was going to happen next?

The Tea Act   Nearly the entire English tea trade once belonged to the East India Tea Company, which made it a highly profitable business. But things had changed over time. Much of the tea being consumed in the colonies was Dutch tea, which was being smuggled. The East India Tea Company was in poor condition because of this loss of trade. Then, in the spring of 1773, Parliament decided to correct this situation. They changed the rules for tea trade.

Parliament gave the East India Tea Company the exclusive right to import tea into the colonies. The company would go to the Far East to get the tea, sell it to English wholesalers, who paid a tax, who would then sell it to colonial distributors, who would pay an import tax. The East India Tea Company, through Parliament, would select a few colonial merchants to act as their distributors of the tea. The tea distributors would then sell the tea to local merchants for sale to the colonists. Though it seems complicated, this system was actually simpler than the one which had previously existed.

Parliament had given a monopoly in tea trade to a company of their choosing. By controlling all aspects of the trade, England could see if any other tea was being sold, confiscate it, and sell only the approved tea while collecting the taxes they wanted. The colonial companies who previously sold tea were now locked out of the tea trade. Only those few colonial companies approved by the East India Tea Company would remain in the tea business; the others were simply out of luck.

Parliament believed that the new system would be acceptable to the colonists, since they removed many of the middlemen previously involved in the trade. The price of tea, including the three penny tax, was actually lower than it had ever been. Parliament reasoned if they controlled all the tea sold, a lower tax rate would still provide more income to England since so much more tea than before would be sold legally.

American middlemen in the tea trade were furious. The East India Tea Company would select only a few colonial merchants to act as their agents in the tea trade. Most of the colonial middlemen were going to be put out of business. The Tea Act created a whole new problem: could Parliament hand out a monopoly of tea trade at its pleasure? What would stop it from developing other monopolies of colonial trade?

The real price of this new tea system became apparent to many in the colonies: accepting the new system meant allowing Parliament total control of colonial commerce in the future. Once this was realized, opposition to the Tea Act became strong.

The Boston Tea Party   By the summer of 1773, the colonies were preparing for something to happen. John Hancock smuggled in over 1,000,000 pounds of tea to be stored and sold later. He was preparing for a fight over the tea.

In London, American ships refused to carry tea to the colonies. Only English ships were used. Opposition was so strong that in New York and Philadelphia, ships carrying tea were ordered back to England and their cargo was refused. Most of the colonial governors would not take a stand on either side.

Parliament declared that the tea would be unloaded, even if it was by military force.

In Boston the situation was slightly different. The colonists opposed the unloading of the tea but Governor Hutchinson wanted it done. On November 27, 1773 the British ship, the *Dartmouth*, arrived in Boston Harbor to unload its cargo of tea.

The Boston Tea Party   On December 16, Sam Adams' group, the Sons of Liberty, dressed as Indians, boarded the ships in Boston Harbor, and dumped the ships' cargo of tea into the harbor while thousands along the wharf cheered. *Library of Congress*

Sam Adams used this opportunity to raise the colonists' level of opposition. He held public meetings to arouse the colonists. For days, Adams used every opportunity to stir the fires of discontent. On December 16, Adams' group, the Sons of Liberty, dressed as Indians, boarded the ships, and dumped the tea into Boston Harbor while thousands along the wharf cheered.

The Sons of Liberty had a "tea party." Many wanted to burn the *Dartmouth* just as the colonists in Rhode Island had done to the *Gaspee*, but Adams persuaded them not to. It was not that he felt it wrong. He was afraid that the fire could spread along the wharf and then into the town, hurting their homes and shops.

Paul Revere was a silversmith in Boston. He was also a radical and one of Sam Adams' closest advisors. The day after the "Boston Tea Party," Revere mounted his horse and carried word of the incident to New York, New Jersey and then Pennsylvania. Even John Adams, who detested mob action, rejoiced at the tea party. For weeks afterward, Boston Harbor was brown from the tea.

Governor Hutchinson was furious. When news of this criminal action reached London, Parliament decided it was time to teach the colonists a lesson.

The Intolerable Acts   Parliament could not understand the total breakdown of law and authority in Boston. It was clear that Governor Hutchinson had been blocked in every way he turned; he had lost the respect of those against the protests and lost any possible cooperation with those taking part in the protests. The government in London finally removed him as governor.

Parliament saw that the colonial juries would never convict those who committed this act of violence. They remembered how those accused in the burning of the *Gaspee* were not convicted when put on trial. Parliament was not willing to let the colonists get away with such disregard for property. Something had to be done.

In March 1774 Parliament passed three coercive acts. The first, the Port Act of 1774, closed Boston Harbor until the citizens of Boston paid for the destroyed tea. The second, the Administration of Justice Act, transferred criminal cases outside of Massachusetts until the Governor determined that fair and impartial trials with honest convictions could be achieved. The third act, the Massachusetts Government Act, reorganized the colony's charter. It made the office of the governor more powerful. It caused the local town meetings to have little authority, and it had the state council appointed instead of elected. Finally it altered the method of jury selection.

At the same time Parliament was approving the new measures against the Boston colony, in March of 1774, another ship arrived in Boston loaded with tea. It too was boarded and its contents emptied into the harbor. Had Parliament known about this ship, there would have been additional actions taken to prevent lawlessness in Boston.

When news of the new acts of Parliament arrived on the American shores, Sam Adams used his Committees of Correspondence to spread the word and the objections. He said that Parliament didn't care about justice or why else would they punish the entire colony when only a few took part in the actions? The closing of Boston Harbor would hurt the entire colony. Their historical rights to trial by jury and selection of representatives had been removed. Adams let every other colony know it could happen to them.

Lord North directed the actions only against Massachusetts in order that the other colonies see the error of their ways and reform. Boston was to be an example. Although North viewed the colonies as separate units, by now many of the colonies were no longer feeling that way. Now they were willing to work together.

☆☆

In May 1774, General Gage arrived to take control of Boston. He had been appointed military governor of Massachusetts. Gage had his orders read aloud to the legislature as he took over as the replacement for Hutchinson. Military rule was now the order of the day. The Massachusetts charter was virtually canceled, and the colony was under the direct rule of crown. This was the end to self-government.

Gage set forth his plan. They were to round up the ringleaders of the "Tea Party," arrest them, and ship them to London for trial. He called for a new legislature and rejected those he didn't want. John Adams was one of many who was no longer allowed to remain in the legislature. The will of the people would no longer be considered. Boston was under military rule.

Things grew worse in Boston as General Gage tried to enforce the new laws. The Port Act had put thousands out of work. The people became troubled as hard times fell on the entire colony. Even those who did not support the radicals could not support this bill. Gage found he had almost no support from the citizens of Boston.

One by one, leaders in the different colonies saw the need to meet and discuss a common plan of action. Both Sam and John Adams called for a meeting of all the colonies in newspaper articles. Their cry was echoed by the New York Committee of Correspondence, which publicly called for a meeting.

The Virginia colony experienced a conflict of their own, since their protest against Parliament caused their legislature to clash with the Governor of Virginia. Now Thomas Jefferson also called for a Continental Congress to unify the colonies into action. By the summer of 1774, from one end of the American colonies to the other, the colonies called for a meeting in Philadelphia in September 1774.

The radicals in Boston were not willing to wait to see if a congress would do anything. Sam Adams and John Hancock formed a Committee of Public Safety in Boston. They declared publicly that their group was being organized to help protect the colony from Indians. The reality was that they used these committees of safety to form, train, and supply local militias. Their committees began collecting and storing guns, powder, and other military equipment for war.

The First Continental Congress

★☆★☆★☆★☆★☆★☆★☆★☆★☆★☆★☆★☆★

To help Virginia's delegates to the First Continental Congress, Thomas Jefferson put together a pamphlet of instructions. It was intended as little more than a few notes for the Virginia delegation, but the members of the delegation were so impressed by its clear direction and reasoning that they had Jefferson's pamphlet published without asking his permission.

The purpose of "A Summary View of the Rights of British America" was to lay out a plan to reform the way Parliament and the King were treating the colonies. Though not designed to help establish a new nation, Jefferson's declaration of the natural rights of man made it seem clear that the colonies were being ill treated by the government in England. For many, this pamphlet convinced them that a new nation was the only real choice.

Jefferson hoped that the colonies could establish a new relationship with England, one similar to the relationship that existed between England and Scotland. The colonies would be an independent nation, equal to England, all with a common king, and become a member of the Commonwealth of Great Britain.

The publication of his pamphlet on both sides of the Atlantic Ocean, quickly moved Thomas Jefferson to the forefront in the fight for independence.

In September of 1774, representatives from all the colonies except Georgia, met in Philadelphia for the First Continental Congress. Many of those who attended the Stamp Act Congress also came to Philadelphia. Among those in attendance were Robert Livingston of New York, John Rutledge from South Carolina, and Edward Tilghman and Caesar Rodney of Maryland. Virginia, the largest of all the colonies, was represented by among others, Richard Henry Lee, and George Washington.

For many, it was the first real contact they had with citizens from other colonies. It was a time for getting to know one other and for seeing what they were all about.

John Hancock, a wealthy shipper, was selected as president of the Congress. His prior involvement with the Sons of Liberty and Committees of Correspondence made him acceptable to the radicals, while his wealth and position in Boston's community made him acceptable to the conservative group in Congress.

Views of all types were discussed. Some suggested that the colonies take a closer look at their actions, because England had the right to do what it had done. These individuals viewed the actions of many of the colonists as being against the law. Still, a few others asked for a total break with England. Most of the delegates viewed the recent events as serious matters which could be resolved without war.

Joseph Gallway of Pennsylvania went so far as to suggest that the Congress request Parliament establish a President General to preside over the colonies and allow them limited self rule. Gallway suggested Parliament would keep veto power over the laws of the colonies. Few of the delegates were ready for this type of sugges-

John Hancock *John Hancock, a wealthy colonial merchant, was an early leader in the revolutionary cause. Involved with the Committees of Correspondence and the Sons of Liberty, Hancock was selected as the president of the Second Continental Congress. He is famous for his large signature on the Declaration of Independence. Library of Congress*

tion. The Congress passed a series of grievances and resolutions, condemning Parliament's actions against the colonies.

They agreed to boycott or stop buying English goods and shipping materials to England. But they could not agree on anything else about their boycott. Could they purchase products from other British colonies such as the Bahamas or Canada? Could they sell to them as well? When should this boycott begin? Each colony wanted something different. Getting all thirteen colonies to work together was going to be a difficult job.

They were able to agree on one other important matter. They recommended to the counties in Massachusetts, "arm yourselves and resist tyranny."

After five weeks of meetings, in October 1774, the delegates decided to go back to their colonies to talk to the leaders there and let them know the different ideas which were discussed. They agreed to return to Philadelphia in May 1775 for a Second Continental Congress.

By telling the citizens of Boston to resist tyranny and arm themselves, in effect, the First Continental Congress gave their approval for war. Although they did not realize it, this was the beginning of the American Revolution.

Part Two

The War For Independence

The Fighting Begins

★☆★☆★☆★☆★☆★☆★☆★☆★☆★☆★☆★☆★☆★☆★☆★

Lexington and Concord   In January of 1775, England sent word to the military commanders in the colonies that the force of the military was now to be used against any of the colonists who went against English law. It was early April before word of this reached Boston Harbor, and it did not take long for the military commander to act.

General Gage was aware that the Committees for Public Safety were just a front for the colonists to arm themselves. Now with London's permission, he was going to put a stop to the colonists resistance to law and order.

First he wanted to arrest the ring leaders. After the First Continental Congress adjourned, Sam Adams and John Hancock returned to Massachusetts to continue their efforts in building up the militia. General Gage's first orders were to find these two men and arrest them.

As these orders were issued, Gage proceeded to plan his first action. He would march his troops out of Boston to the nearby community of Concord, Massachusetts to confiscate the arms and ammunition gathered by the colonists.

What Gage did not know was that the patriots had spies working in the British military headquarters. After the patriot leaders learned of Gage's plan, they agreed to warn the local militias with a signal when the British soldiers were to move out from Boston. But how would they come? The British could leave Boston by boat or road. The choice of the British would determine their target.

The roads out of Boston were now being guarded by British soldiers, so it was decided that a signal must be used that could be seen across the Charles River. On the night of April 18, 1775, as the British soldiers prepared to move out from Boston, the warning signal was given.

It was decided that from the top window in the steeple of Christ's Church in Boston, a light signal was to be given. One lamp was to be lit if the British were leaving by land, two lamps to indicate they were leaving by sea.

Suddenly late that night, two lamps were placed in the window. Across the river, the signal was seen by Paul Revere. Along with Dr. Samuel Prescott and Sam Dawes, Paul Revere rode out into the black night calling for the men to prepare, for "*the British are coming*!" The local militia was given the advance warning it needed.

By the time the British arrived at Lexington, Massachusetts, a colonial militia training area on the way to Concord, the local militia was waiting. The British were met on an open field in Lexington by the local militiamen, known as minutemen. They were called "minutemen" because they could be ready to fight with their muskets at a minute's notice.

The British army arrived to find about 70 minutemen armed and waiting for them. Each army stood in formation facing each other, not more than sixty feet apart. Neither side was willing to move out of the way of the other. Also, neither side was willing to make the first move against the other army. Then came the "shot heard around the world."

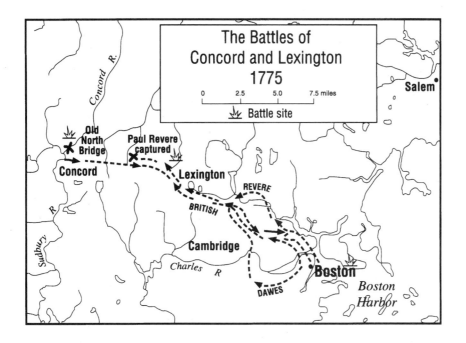

The Battles of
Concord and Lexington
1775

0   2.5   5.0   7.5 miles

⚔ Battle site

Salem

Old
North
Bridge

Paul Revere
captured

Concord

Lexington

REVERE

BRITISH

Cambridge

Charles R.

Boston

Boston
Harbor

DAWES

Concord R.

Sudbury

Someone fired a musket from off the green. No one knows who fired the first shot, but the response was immediate. The British army and the colonial militia opened fire on each other. In a matter of moments, eight minutemen lay dead while another ten were wounded. That first shot was the start of the war which would forever change the relationship of England and its American colonies. The Battle of Lexington and Concord had begun.

The British soldiers chased off the remaining American militiamen and proceeded to search the homes and barns for military supplies. Finding nothing, the British army continued its mission and moved towards Concord.

The militia followed the British to Concord. As they followed the British army, their numbers grew as more and more men arrived to help. Before long, the American colonists had an entire army. Once at Concord, the British destroyed what little supplies and arms they could find. Most of the supplies had been already carried off in the night by the colonial militia, to be hidden elsewhere. As the British army began its return trip to Boston, it was followed by the minuteman army. The British were going to be in for a long difficult march home.

Frontier life had taught the local militiamen much, and they used the same techniques against the British that the Indians had used against them. The British were called "Redcoats" because of the bright red uniform jackets worn by the soldiers. As the minutemen followed the British army back to Boston, the bright red coats made it easy to spot the English soldiers from hiding places along the way. The minutemen fired into the marching soldiers from behind cover and then ran away to the next hiding position.

This tactic was devastating to the English troops, killing and wounding many. By the time the British returned to Boston, they were discouraged. They returned to Boston without the arms and ammunition they had expected to capture. Now the colonial militia surrounded the town, trapping them. No one knew it then, but the colonial army was to stay and surround Boston for nearly one full year.

For a short time, the Massachusetts minutemen stood alone against the Empire which had defeated France and Spain in war. But as word spread of the fighting which had occurred, Connecticut, Rhode Island, and New Hampshire all sent troops to help. In all, well over 3,000 men came to help the patriots defend liberty.

Events moved fast. For many of the delegates, the trip to Philadelphia would take several weeks and they began their journey in early April. While many were on the road traveling to Philadelphia, Massachusetts changed the course of the meeting to come. As the delegates gathered, the war was already upon them.

Word of the fighting at Lexington and Concord greeted the delegates as they reached Philadelphia. By the time the Second Continental Congress got under way, many of the delegates felt that a full war with England was unavoidable. Still, many others hoped for a peaceful solution. George Washington, like many others, could see that war with the mother country was already here.

As the delegates continued to gather, a small fort, named Ticonderoga, on the route to Canada in New York, was attacked by Ethan Allen and his "Green Mountain Boys." The Green Mountains Boys were an army begun nearly thirteen years before in Vermont. The colonies of New York and Massachusetts both claimed Vermont as part of their colony. When each tried to tax Vermont, the Green Mountain Boys offered armed resistance to tax collection. It might be said that Vermont had been fighting for its own independence for thirteen years. Ethan Allen hoped that by securing Fort Ticonderoga for the 13 colonies, they would be more willing to grant Vermont independence from New York and Massachusetts.

In May 1775, by merely walking up to Fort Ticonderoga at night and knocking on the door, Allen and his army captured the entire fort. The fort was not prepared for an attack, and before anyone in the fort could realize what was happening, Ethan Allen and his army rushed in through the opened gate. The entire British unit was captured with only a single soldier injured. The fort's supplies were captured and taken for the use of the colonial army. Colonel Benedict Arnold, of Massachusetts was sent to help in the capture of the fort.

Who would claim the captured supplies? It was decided that the Continental Congress would now handle the question. Some supplies were sent to Boston, the rest held back for future use. For the moment, the colonial army surrounding Boston was given its needed supplies.

Now Congress had to deal with the fighting in Boston and the status of Vermont. The issue of Vermont was put aside because no one wanted to offend either New York or Massachusetts. If war was to come, both colonies would be needed to help. Vermont was going to have to wait.

It was widely known that Washington was one of the few colonial leaders with any military experience. As the Congress debated what to do, Washington wore his uniform from the French and Indian War daily to his seat in Congress. It was his way of showing the other delegates that it was time to begin the war in earnest and that he wanted to be named Commander-in-Chief of the army.

John Adams of Massachusetts, among other delegates, proposed that Washington be named the Commander-in-Chief of an army formed from soldiers from all the colonies. His selection would help to tie the middle and southern colonies to the fighting, which was already occurring in the north. A southern commander would also bring troops from his home and neighboring colonies. It would make the army truly a continental army.

The delegates voted to select George Washington as the Commander of the Continental Army. It was unanimous: Washington would lead the American forces. Unknown to the delegates in Philadelphia, on the very day a new commander had been selected the Battle of Bunker Hill in Boston was being fought.

Once Congress selected a commander, it needed to decide on a plan of action for the army. There were more British colonies to the north and not everyone in Canada liked the British. Congress quickly agreed on General Washington's plan to attack the British army in Canada. They hoped those in Canada opposed to British rule would help the thirteen American colonies in their fight against the British government. Generals Philip Schuyler and Richard Montgomery were selected to head the invasion force. As Washington prepared to leave for Boston, Schuyler and Montgomery prepared for the American invasion of Canada.

John Adams *Slow to join the revolutionary cause, by the early 1770's, Adams became one of the most outspoken leaders against British rule. He was instrumental in both the writing and passage of the Declaration of Independence. Library of Congress*

It is important at this point to say something about women's roles during this critical period. Only men were allowed to serve in Congress, since it was considered undignified for a woman to be involved in politics. Many of the male leaders also believed politics too complicated for women to understand. Yet many women such as Abigail Adams, the wife of John Adams, held a great influence in the affairs of their husbands. Abigail functioned not only as the head of the family in John's absence, running their farm and handling all their personal matters, but she was also John's conscience. Often political ideas were worked out through the correspondence between John and Abigail, long before John would make mention of them to his colleagues in Congress.

In particular, as the colonial army struggled for survival around Boston, Abigail Adams organized the women of Boston in support of the militia. The women collectively made saltpeter, used in the making of gunpowder, and melted lead into molds, making bullets for the soldiers to use. Carrying supplies to the men on the front lines during battle, these women often made the difference between a loss or a victory. Finally, there are many stories of women, such as Debra Samson of Massachusetts, who disguised themselves and served as soldiers, fighting alongside men in battle.

Battle of Bunker Hill Meanwhile as Congress selected Washington to head the Continental Army, the British were determined to break through the colonial militia which encircled Boston. They decided to cross the Charles River and make their move against the colonials on Breed's Hill. The Continental Army, as it was now called, used nearby Bunker Hill as their defensive position. They established a hospital for their wounded and a supply area there. As the British began their move, the minutemen moved to nearby Breed's Hill to fight.

The Continental Army was prepared because of the lack of security within British headquarters. The American army had spies in the British headquarters. Three days before the planned British attack, the leaders of the army surrounding Boston were given detailed information concerning the British attack. The colonial army had time to prepare, knowing where and when the British attack would occur. The British lost the advantage of surprise.

The Battle of Bunker Hill *Wet, muddy and in a very weak position, the British had to march uphill against the attack of colonial musket fire. Fearing a trap, the British were unable to follow up their success on Breed's Hill and withdrew. Library of Congress*

The British army crossed the river, and after leaving their boats, had to get out in marsh land. Carrying fully loaded backpacks and supplies, the soldiers had to walk through deep mud to take up their attacking formations. Wet, muddy and in a very weak position, the British had to march uphill against the attack of colonial musket fire.

After fierce fighting, the British army made the colonial militia withdraw to Bunker Hill. But it was only after the colonial ammunition and supplies had run out.

Had the British realized that this was the reason for withdrawal, the conflict could have ended there with one more British attack. All that the British army needed to do was to continue the fighting to Bunker Hill for a complete victory. Instead, fearing that they might be falling into a trap, the British soldiers withdrew.

This victory, if it could be called that, was too costly for the British. Over 1,000 of its 2,200 man army were killed, while colonial army deaths were only 400. More importantly, the Continental Army proved it could stand up to the "greatest fighting army in the world," the British army. This gave hope and the feeling of success to the new army.

The result of this battle was more than just raised spirits. It caused members of both sides of the conflict to realize that a negotiated settlement was going to be more difficult to accomplish. Many in the colonies now came to the belief that the time for talk had passed and there was only one choice—*WAR!*

Washington Takes Command   By early July 1775, Washington arrived in Massachusetts, just outside of Boston. He immediately began to organize his army. He began their training, while they remained ready to attack the British in Boston. Even before Washington's appointment as military leader, several colonies sent men to Boston to help; it was now up to Washington to turn these men into an army.

The colonial army surrounded the city of Boston and a siege attack began. They would keep the British trapped by blocking all the land routes out of Boston.

Washington realized that even though it seemed that the British were trapped in Boston, his army could wind up in a trap. If the British sent an army from Canada, his army would become trapped between the Canadian army and the one in Boston. He now prayed for the success of Schuyler and Montgomery.

The War Expands

☆☆☆☆☆☆☆☆☆☆☆☆☆☆☆☆☆☆☆☆☆☆☆☆☆

George Washington sent Colonel Benedict Arnold to assist in the invasion of Canada. Arnold had been with Ethan Allen at Ticonderoga and had seized needed arms for the Continental Army surrounding Boston. Arnold's military ability was going to be needed to the north.

Montreal had been French, and many of the French Canadians were unhappy about British rule. Congress hoped that by sending an army into Canada, the French Canadians would take up arms to rid themselves of their British rulers and fight alongside the Continental Army.

In late August 1775, the Continental Army set out to win Canada to the American cause. The army began its operation at the recently captured Fort Ticonderoga, located on Lake George in New York. They intended to use the fort as their supply base. Problems plagued the army from the start, since they found handling the water route along the lake too difficult.

Instead, they pushed through the wilderness. Taking supplies and artillery through unbroken territory was a task the army was not up to. With no paths to cross, dragging artillery through the forest slowed the army and tired it out. Sickness ravaged the troops as their supplies ran out.

As Arnold moved north through New York, General Montgomery was moving northwest from Maine. After a short siege, St. John, along the route to Montreal, was captured for the Americans. However, the British commander, General Carleton, was able to escape.

As Arnold's army continued its northward journey, Arnold sent a letter to General Schuyler to indicate his position and the plan to attack Montreal. The Indian messenger sent to deliver the message to General Schuyler took the letter directly to General Carleton. Now the British knew the plan and would be ready.

Arnold met General Montgomery at the St. Lawrence River on December 21, 1775. Together, they advanced towards Montreal in a blinding snowstorm. By the end of December, the two Generals were ready to attack with nearly 1,000 men.

On December 31, 1775, the American forces attacked the British in Canada. In fierce fighting, Montgomery was killed, Arnold wounded, and over 500 American soldiers were killed or captured. The attack fell apart soon after it had begun. The British were well prepared for the attack. If not for Arnold's letter to General Schuyler, the attack might have been successful.

The plan to attack the British at Montreal and capture it was a dismal failure. It took the Continental Army longer to reach Canada than expected and their supplies ran short. Though the plan was good, the British army was prepared and much stronger than expected. The Continental Army suffered its first major loss.

While a British army was spending the winter in Boston, another British army in Canada was preparing to make its move down from Canada. When spring thaw came, the British moved ships and men from Canada into upper New York. What little remained of the

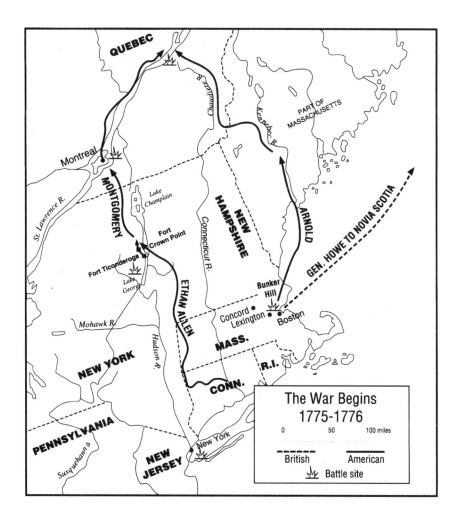

The War Begins
1775-1776

0   50   100 miles

---- British   ——— American

🔆 Battle site

American invading force was chased out of Canada. The few American gunboats and canoes were wiped out by British ships on the St. Lawrence and on the lakes. Yet, even with the repelling of the American forces, the British were unable to destroy the army. Even with loyalists joining the British to fight, additional troops from England were going to be needed everywhere.

As the spring of 1775 warmed into summer, few American soldiers remained in northern New York State. General Arnold was forced to escape southward with whatever soldiers he had. Fort Ticonderoga and all of the lakes of northern New York were back in British hands.

Meanwhile, time passed slowly for Washington, giving him the chance to organize and train the Continental Army around Boston. After sitting out the winter in Boston and trying to recover after their loss at Bunker Hill, the British left Boston in March of 1776. On March 18, Washington led the troops into Boston. The Continental Army had won, and Washington planned on doing it again!

1776 • Independence and the Battle for New York

☆☆☆☆☆☆☆☆☆☆☆☆☆☆☆☆☆☆☆☆☆☆☆☆☆☆

In April 1776, Washington left Boston for New York. He understood two important requirements to win this war. First, as long as the army remained intact as a fighting force, there would be hope; and second, the colonies were going to need help. He immediately set out to have Congress get help for the American cause.

Washington began to oversee the defense of New York City. By the summer, the British had sent ships and men to Staten Island in New York Harbor. The Howe brothers, Richard an admiral, and William, a general, were determined to end this colonial nonsense. Together, they would stop this colonial upstart named Washington. Meanwhile, Washington was in New York Harbor on Long Island (this section is now Brooklyn). Both armies were preparing for battle when Washington received joyful news from Philadelphia.

Declaration of Independence   Among the new members who had recently come to the Second Continental Congress in

Philadelphia was a Virginian named Thomas Jefferson. His pamphlet, "A Summary View of the Rights of British America," had become well known among the delegates. In it, Jefferson spoke out against King George III and argued the need for a drastic change in America. He was calling for independence though he did not want to say it directly. Not all the delegates would stand for such a statement at that time.

Slowly the radicals in Congress were winning over those members who were more moderate, and action was being taken to cut the ties with England. In March of 1776, the news of the success of the American forces surrounding Boston had reached the Congress. George Washington had given the Americans their first major victory, and the spirits of Congress soared. Now Congress was ready to take the next step.

As Jefferson returned to the Continental Congress on May 4, 1776, the Congress declared that the American ports were open to all ships except the British. America would no longer be restricted to trade with Britain alone; America would buy and sell goods to anyone who would be its friend.

On the very day Jefferson returned to the Continental Congress, Virginia declared itself to be a free and independent state, established a new government, and authorized its delegates in the Continental Congress to propose that all the colonies declare themselves a free and independent nation.

With the urging of Sam and John Adams, on May 15, 1776, the Virginian delegation rose to propose that the colonies declare themselves a free and independent nation.

The Continental Congress had been moving in this direction for a long time and now Congress was faced with taking action. Not all the members of the Second Continental Congress were in favor of this move. Many wanted a reconciliation with England,

Thomas Jefferson *His ability to write clearly and persuade his readers to his point of view, led Jefferson to the front of the Colonial political writers. As a member of the Second Continental Congress, he was the author of the Declaration of Independence. The Library Company of Philadelphia*

believing that recent events were a temporary setback; they believed loyalty to the crown was still in the hearts of the people.

Congress understood that to declare themselves a free and independent nation meant war. Once done, there would be no chance of a negotiated peace.

If all the colonies in Congress could not agree to separate from England, those colonies remaining loyal to England would be forced to fight against the other colonies. Therefore, Congress decided to prevent brother from fighting brother; the decision for independence had to be unanimous.

Many of the delegates in Congress were not authorized or were unwilling or unable to take such action. In order to give time for the delegates to send for instructions, John Adams requested that time be allotted to create a declaration stating what the colonies were doing and why. Those against independence saw this as just a tactic to put off the vote on independence, because they said Adams knew it would not pass. They were correct, and the debate went on for two days. Finally, Congress decided to put off the vote for independence for three weeks until a declaration stating the aims and reasons for their actions could be written.

The next day, Congress established a committee of five men to write this declaration. The committee for the Declaration consisted of Thomas Jefferson, John Adams of Massachusetts, Benjamin Franklin of Pennsylvania, Robert Livingston of New York, and Roger Sherman of Connecticut.

The committee of five met to decide who would write this document. Franklin, Livingston and Sherman quickly pointed out that they had no experience in writing political documents and would only make a mess of it. It came down to Adams or Jefferson. Adams would later recall the discussion, stating that Jefferson asked him to write it and Adams refused saying Jefferson should write it. When Jefferson pushed Adams for his reason, Adams remembered saying "Reason first—You are a Virginian, and a Virginian ought to appear at the head of this business. Reason second—I am obnoxious, suspected, and unpopular. You are very much otherwise. Reason third—You can write ten times better than I can." Adams' view of the discussion cannot be far from the truth, because Jefferson, in his own diary, described their conversation the same way. Jefferson added his response, "Well, if you are decided, I will do as well as I can." The other members of the committee also recalled the discussion in a very similar manner.

It was decided: Thomas Jefferson would write their Declaration of Independence. Jefferson worked long and hard and came up with what he believed was the finest writing he had ever done. The committee agreed, making only two or three minor corrections or comments. On June 28, 1776, Jefferson submitted his Declaration of Independence to the Continental Congress.

The document was simple in nature; Jefferson hoped to clearly state the reasons for the need for independence. He believed that by describing the injustices done, the world would have to agree with the decision made.

The Declaration of Independence had four main points. First, to convince the world of the justification and right of the colonies to separate from the mother country. Second, to show that governments are established with the consent of the governed. When a government becomes destructive, the people have a right and duty to change the government and create a new one if needed. He said, "The purpose of any government is to guarantee the people the right to "*Life, Liberty, and the Pursuit of Happiness.*" Jefferson believed that this was a moral truth no one could deny. Third, to list the things the King had done to justify their anger. The Declaration of Independence ignored Parliament because the colonies declared that Parliament never had any legal authority over them. Finally, it concluded that to throw off a tyrannical government for a fair and just one was more than justified. Jefferson's document declared **"that these United Colonies are and of right ought to be free and independent states."**

Jefferson said, **"It was intended to be an expression of the American mind, and to give to that expression, the proper tone and spirit called for by the occasion."** He believed the Declaration

Writing the Declaration of Independence *The committee of five, Thomas Jefferson, John Adams, Benjamin Franklin, Robert Livingston, and Roger Sherman meet to review Jefferson's final draft of the Declaration of Independence. The Library Company of Philadelphia*

of Independence summarized the feelings which the Americans had developed, slowly, over the past one hundred years.

Beginning on July 2, the Continental Congress began the debate over Jefferson's document. Each colony seemed to have something to say. Jefferson included a paragraph describing the King as having waged *"a cruel war against human nature,"* having made war on a people having done him no harm and then carried them off. Here, Jefferson referred to slavery.

Jefferson was trapped by the eighteenth century; slavery was an accepted form of labor, supported by religious and scientific beliefs. Jefferson did not believe the Black was of an equal ability as the White; yet he felt slavery was cruel and unjust. But, he, too, was a prisoner of his times, for Jefferson himself owned many slaves. All the southern and middle states demanded this paragraph be removed.

Changes were made to the document's style as well. Quietly sitting by, he saw Congress weaken his document. The radicals knew if they did not give in on certain points, they would never be able to get a unanimous consent to independence. Jefferson realized that to hold the document together as he had written it would preserve his ideas, but kill the freedom he sought.

With all the changes made, the Continental Congress passed the Declaration of Independence on July 4th. The colonies were a free and independent nation, the United States of America. That is, as long as they could win their freedom through war.

The declaration was sent to be printed and was then read publicly on July 8, 1776. It took years before this document became the well known document we think of today; yet, on July 4th when the Continental Congress passed Jefferson's document, John Adams, in his diary, declared that future generations of Americans will celebrate this day with festivals and regard this document with the highest esteem.

Bolstered by the news that the Second Continental Congress passed a Declaration of Independence, Washington was now leading an army of a new nation.

No longer were they fighting just to win a few rights from a mother country. Now it was a war for independence. A new hope and purpose filled Washington and his army, the Army of the United States of America. By August, more and more British soldiers and Hessian mercenaries were in New York Bay as the British prepared to destroy the American army. The Hessians were German soldiers hired by the British government to fight for England.

Washington continued to build up his army, since he knew that an engagement would occur shortly between the two forces. Washington fortified the Brooklyn Heights, building barricades and other defensive positions.

Over 100 British ships delivered men and equipment to Staten Island in New York Harbor. General Howe's army grew large and well equipped. Still, he waited through the spring and summer. He made no move against Manhattan or Washington's army.

Washington was facing overwhelming odds. The Continental Army was unable to hold Breed's Hill against lesser odds, yet Washington believed he could hold off the British advance. Washington split his army in two, keeping half with him in Brooklyn and the other half was sent across the East River to Manhattan. Now his army was divided, with the East River separating the two parts. In between, the British navy controlled the waterways.

On August 21, 1776, the British army landed in Brooklyn and began to move on the American lines. By the end of the day, over 15,000 men landed in south Brooklyn ready to fight. Bad weather held off the British attack till the 25th.

The battle took place on the flatlands of Brooklyn. The British overwhelmed the American army. The American troops took too

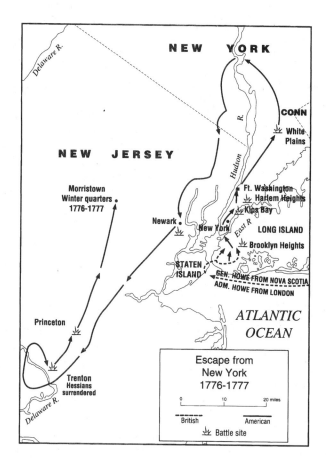

The following is a map titled:

Escape from
New York
1776-1777

long reloading their muskets and this gave the British troops time
to charge. The muskets of the American Army had no bayonets and
so they were unprepared for hand to hand combat. The Americans
fled the field, leaving their artillery for the advancing British army.

After a few hours of intense fighting, the superior numbers of
the British quickly forced Washington to withdraw. There was one
bright spot for the American army during the withdrawal: Maryland
troops unexpectedly attacked the British on their flank and held
them off while the Americans retreated. By noon of that day, the
American troops were behind the works built on Brooklyn Heights.

They were looking over the East River to Manhattan and the rest of the American army. Meanwhile, General Howe rested with his troops after their victory. He was not going to repeat the error of the British commander at Bunker Hill and charge uphill at fortified earth works. Instead he began to build his own, digging trenches closer and closer to American lines. His troops remained protected behind British defense works. For the next two days it rained, but the British kept digging and getting closer to the American lines.

Finally, after seeing there was no chance of winning a battle, Washington and his army withdrew silently and quickly in the night. The bad weather kept British ships off the river and allowed Washington, on the 28th, to move troops across the river in the dark. Back and forth, small boats ferried the troops as fog covered the retreat. They were able to escape with all their equipment. This time, nothing was left for the British to capture.

The rain and fog kept the American's escape secret until midday of the 29th. The army was saved for now.

As September began, the British moved to the western banks of the East River in Manhattan. Their bright red and blue uniforms could be spotted across the waters as they were ferried. The American troops moved to Harlem Heights in northern Manhattan, as 4,000 men were readied for a British attack.

Barges moved the British troops from Long Island to Manhattan at Kips Bay. Just north of where the British were disembarking were American militiamen. As the British force in Manhattan grew, they quickly turned northward toward the American troops. When confronted by the advance of the British, the American lines fell apart and they ran all the way to Harlem.

Howe again decided to rest his troops. By midday, the British were resting instead of pursuing the broken American troops. Later that day the British marched and took positions in northern Manhattan.

Battle of Harlem Heights   *Washington sent Connecticut rangers, about 100 men, to attack the British infantry. Fighting well, they drew the British into the position he wanted. Standing toe to toe with the British, they fired into the British lines. After a short but intense fight, the British and Hessian troops withdrew giving Washington a victory. Library of Congress*

Washington saw that all was not lost. The next day, he sent Connecticut rangers, about 100 men, to attack the British infantry. They fought well, retreating slowly, drawing the British into the position he wanted. Then, while the British forces were out in the open, Washington sent in the units that ran away the day before. Standing toe to toe with the British, they fired their muskets into the British lines. After a short but intense fight, suddenly the British and Hessian troops withdrew. Washington had a victory.

By mid September a stalemate had developed; the British occupied New York City, while Washington and his army remained less than ten miles to the north. In the name of the American cause, many saboteurs began a campaign to burn the city down. In two days, large portions of the city were burnt. While smoke still rose and embers were hot, the British captured an American spy, Nathan Hale. Feeling extremely angry over the fires, General Howe ordered him to be hanged the next morning. As the noose was placed around Hale's neck, he was allowed to make a last statement. Speaking out for the American cause, Hale ended his statement, "I only regret that I have but one life to lose for my country." With that, Hale was hanged.

☆☆

By early October 1776, the American army was reinforced with troops from New England and General Charles Lee from Virginia. Everyone urged Washington to retreat from Manhattan to White Plains, just a few more miles farther north. The American position was to weak to defend. The British could easily come up behind the American lines by using the Hudson River and their ships.

Seeing the possible trap, Washington moved his army to White Plains. It was a slow and difficult march since the army had no carts and few horses to carry their supplies. The soldiers were burdened with a heavy load, often finding themselves with nothing to eat because they were ahead of the carts carrying their rations. A small force was left behind in Throgs Neck (in the lower Bronx) to delay the British forces which would follow. They did their job, slowing the pursuing British enough for the American troops to complete their withdrawal.

General Howe waited ten days to reorganize his army before pursuing the Americans into White Plains. Washington used local militia for the battle. With the thundering, pounding drums suddenly sounding from the woods, the British cavalry exploded onto the field, terrifying the American army. The militia broke ranks but the rest of the regular army stayed and withdrew slowly with few casualties. Howe missed his target and the American army withdrew to higher ground. October faded into November before further action happened.

Lack of trained military personnel was showing. Could the American army gain the military experience it needed before losing the war? Right now the army just had to survive. Washington realized that he had been lucky in New York. General Howe could have brought ships up the Hudson River behind his lines and forced him to fight on two fronts at the same time. The army would have been trapped in the middle.

General Howe did not do this because he believed it to be unnecessary. After all, he was just fighting an army of colonials. How could they hope to defeat the British army? The British needed to gain experience fighting against the Continental Army as well.

☆☆

While Washington had to deal with General Howe in New York, Charleston, South Carolina also had to deal with British forces. By July of 1776, British warships and transports had gathered outside of Charleston to make a military move on that colony.

The British attempted to land soldiers and equipment. The South Carolina militia resisted. The British did not select the best position to unload troops and supplies. The beach areas selected were under high cliffs looking down on them. The Americans had positioned themselves on high grounds near the water's edge and would shoot down on ships with cannon and muskets. As the British attempted to land and unload, the militia would fire a hail of bullets onto the decks of the ships. All landing attempts failed.

Finally the shallow waters ended the British landing attempts as the British ships ran aground. When the British sailors tried to perform their duties, they were shot by American militiamen on the cliffs. The British fleet was forced to withdraw. It would be several years before South Carolina would be attacked by the British again.

The withdrawing ships and men went to New York.

☆☆

Troops originally sent to Canada were now being diverted to New York. Washington was now facing an army made up of troops from Canada, South Carolina, Boston, and New York. In addition, General Howe was building up the British forces in New Jersey and Pennsylvania.

Howe moved his entire New York force back to Manhattan and Washington and his advisors assumed they were making a move on Fort Lee in New Jersey just across the Hudson River. Before making a move on New Jersey, General Howe took Fort Washington in upper Manhattan, securing New York City for the British.

While the Americans were trying to figure out what Howe would do next, Howe's forces crossed the Hudson River and captured Fort Lee in New Jersey. Washington's army was now divided into three parts. Two on each side of the Hudson River, north of Howe's Army, and the third portion in New Jersey towards the center of that state. Facing a much larger army, Washington had to consolidate his army into one large army.

As November was drawing to a close, General Cornwallis, at the head of another British army, was moving up through New Jersey. But, unlike General Howe, Cornwallis was moving fast to take Washington. In a quick battle, the Americans lost Newark, New Jersey, but were able to pull back. Washington ordered General Lee to cross the Hudson River into New Jersey and join his forces moving south. Not listening to orders, Lee crossed the river slowly and was finally captured, but his army was able to get away to the south. Five hundred men were sent from northern New York, while 1,000 more came up from Philadelphia.

Now Washington had over 6,000 men ready to do battle. It was time for the British to do something which would help him. They decided no army had ever been successful fighting in the winter and so most of the British army was pulled back into winter quarters. A trail of British forts stretched from Princeton, New Jersey to New York City. Those troops which could not be quartered in these outposts were sent to Rhode Island.

As he was rebuilding his forces, Washington crossed over to the west side of the Delaware River in Pennsylvania. The British believed that he, too, was putting his troops into winter quarters. He was not.

On December 25, 1776, in bitter cold weather, Washington and his army recrossed the ice filled Delaware River into New Jersey. Using 60 boats that went back and forth across the waters in the night, the army was moved from one shore to the other. Marching quietly, many of the men wrapped rags around their feet to keep warm and to stop the bleeding because many had no shoes while marching through the snow and ice.

With the guns wet from the morning dampness, the men were ordered to use bayonets to fight. Approaching the town of Trenton, New Jersey, the American soldiers broke into a slow trot to move up quickly. The Hessian troops were beginning to awaken to headaches after a long night of celebrating Christmas. There were few guards posted since they expected no possibility of attack. In a three pronged attack, Washington's forces moved in on the sleepy soldiers.

By the time of the attack, the American muskets had dried out. As they charged into the town, the Continental soldiers created a firing line as the Hessians tried to organize and create their own line. Before the Hessian commanders had a chance to do what they needed, the American soldiers opened fire. The lead officer, who was trying to organize the Hessian Army into a resistance, was killed and the Hessian troops quickly fell into disorder. In less than one hour, Washington captured over 900 prisoners and more importantly, captured needed supplies. Under Washington's direct command, the army was successful.

But even as the Continental Army enjoyed this victory, Washington was facing another crisis. Many of the soldiers were preparing to go home since their enlistment was ending with the coming of the New Year. Many of Washington's best fighting veterans would soon be heading home. Pleading with his men, Washington was able to talk most of his best troops into staying for 6 more weeks, enough time to prepare for their winter encampment.

Cornwallis reacted quickly to the success of the Continental Army, moving 8,000 men to oppose Washington's now 5,000 man army. Just outside of Princeton, New Jersey, the British positioned themselves to destroy Washington and his army. The Americans had to move quietly.

On January 3, 1777, they prepared to escape the British army. Taking every precaution to be silent, the Continental Army began to withdraw. The Americans went so far as to wrap wagon wheels with rags so as not to make any noise. Cornwallis sent two units into Trenton to attack Washington. Washington was not to be found. Cornwallis was not the type of general to sit and wonder why. He immediately realized Washington's action and began to pursue him.

The British army followed the trail left by the Continental Army and met the rear of Washington's forces at Princeton. The two British units caused panic as they swept through the militia at the end of Washington's lines. Another Kips Bay fiasco looked as if it was about to occur, but this time Washington was there. He rallied the army. General Henry Knox moved the artillery into position and began to fire on the British forces. The Americans pulled back into the town, where Captain Alexander Hamilton was waiting with men ready to fire. The British moved into town and Hamilton's men fired. There the battle ended as the Americans troops devastated the advancing British units. The Continental Army won again.

Washington had to keep the army on the move. The main force of the British army was still nearby at Trenton and could fall upon his army at any moment. Washington decided to go to Morristown, New Jersey for the winter. He did not expect Cornwallis to follow him there, because the British army would be too far from its supply lines if they tried.

The American army still survived. The British may have won the battles in New York but they were unable to destroy the Continental Army.

The Americans won in New Jersey. For now, the British army withdrew from New Jersey and returned to New York City for the rest of the winter.

The British soldiers treated the Americans badly wherever they went, believing all the people in the colonies were traitors to the King. In New Jersey, the British army won many friends for the new nation and Washington because the British soldiers harshly treated the colonists. As the six-weekers left to go home, New Jersey provided Washington with supplies and additional men to rebuild his army.

1777 • Philadelphia and the Saratoga Campaign

☆☆☆☆☆☆☆☆☆☆☆☆☆☆☆☆☆☆☆☆☆☆☆☆☆

Philadelphia is Lost   The winter in Morristown gave Washington time to get needed supplies and more men. Slowly he began to rebuild the army. Spring had come and gone before the Continental or British armies took action. Just as the summer was about to begin, the Marquis de Lafayette of France came to help the American cause. He wanted no pay or military rank. He asked only to serve in the cause of liberty. Washington believed that this was the first of the foreign help and that more would soon be coming from France. He was going to have to wait.

That summer General John Burgoyne began moving south from Canada into New York with fresh British troops and a new plan.

In August 1777, General Howe moved his troops and the British fleet from New York to Chesapeake Bay in the middle states. He was attempting to position the army for a move on Philadelphia from the south. The British hoped that by taking the city where the American revolt began, they could break the American spirit and win the war. Washington countered by moving his forces south of Philadelphia to meet the British and block them.

Sick from the short sea voyage to the Chesapeake Bay, Howe had to rest his troops and give them medical attention before any troop movements could occur. It was a very hot summer and the troops traveled on the ships below decks often not getting enough fresh air and exercise. When he was ready, General Howe began moving north.

The two armies met at Brandywine Creek at the Delaware-Pennsylvania border on September 11, 1777. The advance British unit served as a diversion as the main force of the British army attempted to move around to the rear of Washington's troops.

The American front units, when attacked by the lead British units, broke formation and ran towards the rear in panic. Washington, moving quickly, realized that the forward attack was a diversion and sent General Nathanael Greene and his division to aid the troops in the rear. Greene's troops met the British army and held firm before slowly beginning to withdraw in an orderly manner. General Anthony Wayne held the flank for Washington as the fighting continued till dark.

At night, Washington withdrew his forces to Chester, which is just south of Philadelphia. Again in an orderly fashion, Washington reorganized his army for the next fight. He saw which units held firm and which ran. On review, he realized the collapse of lines in the front was due to new troops, untried and untested. They needed the support of battle tried troops. He determined never to make that mistake again. He also saw that his army had truly become the Continental Army of the United States. General Greene from Rhode Island headed a Virginian unit, while General Wayne from Pennsylvania led a New Jersey unit. No longer would there be a question as to whether units from one state would follow the orders of officers from another state. For the first time, Washington realized he had a solid army with which to face the British.

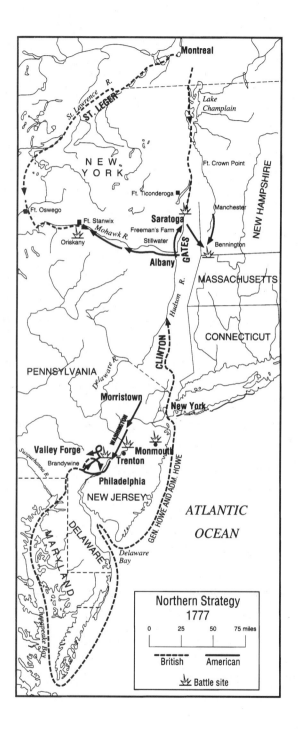

Washington went to Philadelphia to alert the city that the British army was less than 15 miles away. The Continental Congress decided to move the capitol to Lancaster, and then to York, both in western Pennsylvania. The next two days saw heavy rains. All ammunition and guns became wet and unusable as the roads turned to mud. Neither army could move or fight. As the weather cleared, the British army moved forward and took Philadelphia. As they were attempting to secure Philadelphia, they sent out a small unit, which went up along the Schuylkill River to a place called Valley Forge. There the British unit captured large quantities of American supplies, which had been left unguarded.

General Wayne pursued the British but was defeated near the Schuylkill River. The British used bayonets in close hand-to-hand fighting and the Americans were not good at fighting off this type of attack. The American army still needed training in close quarter fighting. With the areas near and around Philadelphia secure, the British then marched into the city.

General Howe captured the birthplace of the American revolt but still was unable to destroy Washington and the American army. It was a British victory without value.

On October 3, 1777, the Continental and British armies met in Mount Airy, Pennsylvania, not far from Philadelphia. The Continental Army overran the British troops in an early morning attack, forcing the British to withdraw quickly. The American army then brought up artillery to increase the attack on the retreating army. The British quickly put together a small stone wall. Moving against a wall was extremely difficult and so General Timothy Pickering decided to demolish the "fort." Artillery was positioned to level it; unfortunately time was wasted, time which could been used to move against the main British force while they were still in panic. The British used this time to regroup.

The early morning fog was thick. Fog mixed with the heavy smoke from the gunpowder, and American units fired at each other, unable to see. General Greene met strong resistance on the British flank. Washington was close to a victory but was unable to hold onto it. That day saw over 1,000 men injured or killed on the American side alone. One fourth of Washington's army was lost.

October drifted into November and Washington and his troops saw little additional action.

Saratoga While Washington was facing the British army in the Philadelphia area, General Burgoyne was bringing another British army south. Before the war began in earnest, Major General John Burgoyne had written a paper for the British High Command in London, "Thoughts For Conducting the War from the Side of Canada." His ideas for conducting the war were accepted in London and he was sent to North America to end the war.

His plan was simple in design. Sweep down from Canada and capture Fort Ticonderoga, Lake Champlain, and Lake George. Then move down along the Hudson River and take Albany. Next, join all British forces and the Mohawk Indians, and together with General Clinton, smash through to New York City, dividing New England from the other colonies and ending the war.

Burgoyne believed Washington would have to move north into New York to defend the region. Once there, the combined British forces would destroy him. If he did not move north to protect New England, supplies would be cut off from the army and he would suffer a shortage of replacement troops. The Continental Army would dry up and wither away from lack of equipment and supplies and men.

Burgoyne soon learned that plan and reality often are not the same. On May 6, 1777, General Burgoyne landed on the shores of the St. Lawrence. His force included German soldiers and supplies. He encountered problems from the beginning. Burgoyne believed he would easily raise a Tory (those loyal to the crown) army. Instead he was barely able to get any support from the people. Next, he planned on a Indian army of several thousand, but less than 400 Indians were sent to help. Then he found that he was unable to buy the needed horses to pull over 100 artillery pieces or the wagons his army required to haul their supplies. General Howe then wrote to him, saying that his forces would be busy in Pennsylvania and he could spare only a few men. Burgoyne's army was less than half of what he expected. He had to change his plan.

Moving south, Burgoyne quickly had his first engagement. He did not understand the Indians or how they could be used most effectively. Burgoyne had the Indians fight alongside the German troops in the woods. The Germans knew nothing about the Indians, and the Indians did not trust the Germans. He soon learned to separate these two groups.

While the British were making a move on Fort Ticonderoga, the Americans fled the fort in the night. The next day saw many small battles taking place. The American soldiers stood their ground but were defeated.

Burgoyne was happy; a large number of prisoners and enemy supplies were captured. Fort Ticonderoga was taken and the area nearby was secured. Burgoyne's original plan called for moving the British army down Lake George by boat, but because of the quick success of his army near Ticonderoga, Burgoyne decided to go over land. His army now had to travel 20 miles through dense forest, pulling artillery where there were no trails.

General Schuyler added to Burgoyne's troubles. He had woodsmen cut trees along the route, blocking the narrow path they were taking. This slowed the British army even more than the forest alone. The Americans moved logs and cut trees along brooks to alter the waters' paths and flood the nearby areas. As small streams were blocked up, water accumulated along the route, making mud and collecting insects and mosquitoes nearby. Progress became very slow.

Burgoyne faced another problem. Drunken Indians attacked a Tory settlement, where they killed and scalped a young woman. She was the fiance of the leader of the Tory militia coming to help Burgoyne. What could he do? If he arrested the guilty Indian and had him executed, the rest of the Indians would leave. If he did nothing, the militia would not come to fight and help! Burgoyne was forced to arrest the guilty Indian.

The one fear that held all the colonists on the frontier together was their fear of savage Indian attacks. The leaders of the American army made the most out of the situation, claiming the British were arming the Indians and sending them out indiscriminately. Many colonists who would have supported the British, now supported the Americans. Food and supplies found their way across the British lines to the American army.

After nearly a month, the British army completed its 20-mile journey through the wilderness. Instead of sending a force ahead to cross the Hudson River and attack Albany, Burgoyne had the troops make camp and waste another month until all the artillery was brought forward to their camp position. In August, Burgoyne received word from General Howe. Howe informed Burgoyne that he was staying to fight in Pennsylvania. However, Howe did wish Burgoyne "Good Luck."

Burgoyne did not let any other commander or officer know Howe was not coming. He was afraid of the effect of the news on his men. He had decided to let the troops know the news after he received the other troops he was expecting. He knew over 1,000 troops were coming from the west in Canada with another 1,000 Indians to fight.

The Americans also knew these 2,000 additional fighting men were moving to support Burgoyne. An American unit from New York unit met this band of British reinforcements along the Mohawk River and engaged them in battle. The British forces were severely hurt, losing much of their equipment and food. Though defeated, the British were able to pull back. It seemed for the moment that they were blocked by the American army.

By mid-August, word was received that General Arnold was coming with 3,500 Continental soldiers to reinforce the New York unit. When the British commander heard this, the British army pulled back again. But this time it was all the way back to Canada. Fear of overwhelming numbers forced the British to give up any plan of attack from the west. Finally Arnold arrived, but with barely 1,000 men. For the British it was too late to worry about the size of Arnold's army; the threat of a British attack from the west was eliminated. Burgoyne was not going to get the additional men from the west. But he did not know this yet.

Burgoyne sent Colonel Baum eastward to Bennington, Vermont. After two weeks, Baum sent word for reinforcements to come to help engage the enemy. Burgoyne sent the men, all in heavy uniforms and full equipment. In hot summer weather, with coats, sabers, and equipment weighing them down, the troops were unable to move swiftly, making progress very slow. On their second day of march, they were hit with heavy rains. With the roads muddy and the reinforcements tired and hot, they spotted a unit moving in their direction. Believing them to be Tories coming to help, the British soldiers, taking no defensive position, let them approach . They were not British supporters; they were American militia.

The militia opened fire on the unprepared British troops and destroyed the unit, much in the same way they had wiped out Baum's unit earlier in the day. Only nine British soldiers survived the fight. Together, the few survivors retreated as quickly as they could. The American militia followed and harassed the British soldiers all the way back. Over 800 crack British troops were eliminated from Burgoyne's army.

Burgoyne greeted the returning troops as though they were victorious. Now his army was short by 800 men. Later that day he learned of the disaster to the 2,000-man army approaching from the west. His army was nearly 2,800 men fewer than he expected and General Howe was not coming from Pennsylvania. Yet, Burgoyne still believed in his plan.

On September 15th, Burgoyne set out again to take Albany. As he moved his army along the river, the British scouting parties and pickets were lost. The Americans were nibbling away at his army. On the 19th, Burgoyne split his army into three parts and moved south.

Then his army was attacked. The artillery was unable to be fired because the men working them were shot before they could load. As new men move forward to fire the cannons, they too were dropped by musket fire. Burgoyne's crack British troops were not doing well against the Americans.

Then the Americans suddenly began to retreat. The signal had been given to the American troops, letting the British gain control and move into the open field fully exposed to fire. Burgoyne's troops marched out into the unprotected open field. The British suffered heavily. Finally the Hessian troops to the left came to assist the British regulars. The Americans pulled back after three hours of fighting. The German troops prevented the total destruction of Burgoyne's army.

Burgoyne declared the battle a victory to his officers even though they lost over 600 men. He just couldn't see what was happening to him and his army.

The British dug in and made camp. Each day American snipers, who were hiding behind trees and in the underbrush, were picking off British soldiers. The British numbers were falling. By October, Burgoyne realized he had no choice but to withdraw to Canada. The American army followed, attacking stragglers and capturing supply wagons when they could. On October 9th, on the way to Fort Ticonderoga, Burgoyne dug in at Saratoga, New York, to rest his men. General Gates and the American Army were not far behind.

Suddenly General John Stark came down from the north, totally blocking Burgoyne. There was no way out for him. After days of negotiations, Burgoyne agreed to surrender. Gates allowed the British to file out and stack their arms. The entire British army under Burgoyne was taken prisoner.

They were first kept in Massachusetts, then held in Virginia, and finally in Pennsylvania. The soldiers remained prisoners till the end of the war.

The Americans captured the supplies which the British took at Fort Ticonderoga, along with many more the British had brought with them.

Fresh from victory in the north, the troops who fought Burgoyne in the Saratoga campaign went south to reinforce Washington.

1778 · Success in New Jersey and on the Frontier

★☆★☆★☆★☆★☆★☆★☆★☆★☆★☆★☆★☆★☆★☆★☆

The victory at Saratoga gave the Continental Congress force behind their request to France for aid. The victory showed the French that the Continental army could defeat an entire British army, not just in a single battle, but in an entire campaign. There truly was hope for the new nation. France agreed.

The King of France agreed to a treaty with the United States of America. The Treaty of Alliance between the two nations was signed in February 1778. France guaranteed the security and independence of the United States. In return the United States promised to aid and secure the French West Indies in the event of war between France and England.

Valley Forge The winter of 1778 proved to be one of the hardest Washington could have expected. His army was camped in an area northwest of Philadelphia known as Valley Forge. The winter came hard and swift. It was January before huts were constructed for all the men. Even with huts, the men suffered shortages of food, clothing, and equipment. Even firewood, to help keep warm, was in short supply.

Washington expected many desertions, but to his delight the army stayed intact through the winter. This devotion to the American cause only strengthened his determination for victory. As the winter was ending, a Polish general came to the camp to assist Washington in any manner he needed.

Washington accepted the generous offer. Baron Von Steuben began training the American army. He spoke no English, and each command given had to be translated before given to the troops. He taught the army how to quickly handle muskets under fire, and how to follow orders in chaos and in retreat. By the end of the spring, Washington's army was now well prepared to face the best of the British troops.

While Von Steuben was training the troops, Martha Washington came up to Valley Forge. Then came the wives of other generals. Lucy Knox and Kitty Greene, together with Mrs. Washington, helped in the hospitals, caring for wounded and sick soldiers.

The winter's activities raised the spirit of the army and created a new hope of victory.

Battle of Monmouth With the Treaty of Alliance between the United States and France in place, French supplies and money began to arrive for the Americans. In May 1778, with new equipment and supplies purchased, Washington's forces grew to over 11,000 men. For the first time, the Continental army outnumbered the British. Washington wanted to attack the British, who were now on the move in New Jersey. Washington held a council with his generals. General Charles Lee, who was exchanged in a prisoner swap that winter, said the American troops could never stand up to the British regulars on an open field. He continued, by saying that they needed to wait to see what the troops could do. Washington was not willing to wait and saw the chance to attack.

In June 1778, Washington moved most of his army across New Jersey. General Lee said it was a disaster in the making and declined to be second in command. Washington was happy with Lee's decision not to lead the army and then gave the command to Lafayette and Wayne. Lee had hoped, by declining the command, that Washington would feel obligated to halt the operation. When it went ahead as planned, Lee then demanded the command he had earlier refused. Washington had no choice but to reinstate him in command of the second unit.

On June 27th, the American army gave a full frontal attack to the British. With no clear winner, the battle progressed to a second day. Lee offered little help. On the 28th, Lee sent General Wayne to attack British lines in the rear and then proceeded to scatter his troops across the field in no apparent pattern. Wayne asked Lee for more troops since he had the British in a bad position and could defeat them. Lee ignored Wayne's request. Wayne was defeating the British, while trying to join up with the American forces to his left and right. Then without reason, Lee ordered a retreat. No one told Wayne of Lee's orders. Wayne was left to defend his army with no support.

The retreating American army was quite orderly when Washington rode forward to them. Furious at Lee for withdrawing with no cause, Washington ordered Lee off the field, removing him from any command. Washington then took command and had the troops reform firing lines.

The army turned around and attacked the British. In 100 degree heat, the battle raged back and forth all day. General Clinton finally retreated from the field of battle, eventually moving his army across New Jersey to Sandy Hook and then back to Staten Island in

New York Harbor. Exhausted, the American army slept where they were on the field. Washington went to sleep under a tree.

The Battle of Monmouth was a draw. General Lee had snatched defeat from the jaws of victory, while Washington was able to come forward and snatch victory from the jaws of defeat.

Up until this time, generals for Washington's army were often picked because of political pressure. Men not qualified to be generals were given that rank to keep a balance between the states. Washington now demanded and received the ability from Congress to select generals based on merit.

Only because General Lee came from the same state of Virginia, was Washington able to court-martial Lee for incompetence on the field. Had Lee been from another state, attempting to put him on trial might have broken the alliance between the thirteen states. Lee received a slight punishment and was later to return to the army.

This was the last time that the entire British army in the New York area and Washington's army ever met in battle. From this time forward, only portions from each met and fought.

During July 1778, Washington sent Alexander Hamilton to talk to the French Commander d'Estaing off the New Jersey coast. Washington wanted the French to attack the British ships. The British were boarding ships after the Battle of Monmouth in the hope of returning to New York City and Staten Island. The French informed Hamilton they would not and could not stay to help. They had to go the French West Indies immediately to help protect that French colony.

Washington was angry. He and most of the Americans did not understand that France and Britain were really fighting a world war. For the French, the American Revolution was only a small part of their fight with England. The two nations were fighting in Asia, the

Caribbean, North America, Europe, along the Atlantic, Pacific, and Indian Oceans, and in the Mediterranean Sea.

The French refusal to assist the American army at first looked as though it hurt the American cause. But, because the French were building up their army and fleet in the Caribbean, British troops were pulled out of New York to go to British Florida. The British wanted to protect their property in Florida; in fact, they felt that they might even need to attack the French fleet. The army facing Washington was now weakened. Each army spent the year recovering.

On The Frontier The colonists never obeyed the Proclamation of 1763 and even as the war began, colonists continued to cross the mountains into the west. The Indians did not trust white settlers who built settlements and homes. Only those who traded were really welcome.

In the years just before the American Revolution, settlers seemed to pour into the Indian territories and take the Indians' land and hunting grounds. Daniel Boone discovered the Indian path across the mountains called the "Wilderness Trail." This trail led through the Cumberland Gap and brought settlers into western Virginia, now Kentucky. Once there, the Indians and settlers did not get along.

When war between the colonies and England began, the British officers in the west used this hatred between Indians and settlers to their advantage. Lieutenant Colonel Henry Hamilton paid the Indians for scalps of white settlers in the Ohio Valley and western territories. This cause great hatred of the Americans towards him.

Major George Rogers Clark of Virginia was assigned the task of planning an attack against the Indians and their British allies. He decided to attack the British at their supply centers in Illinois.

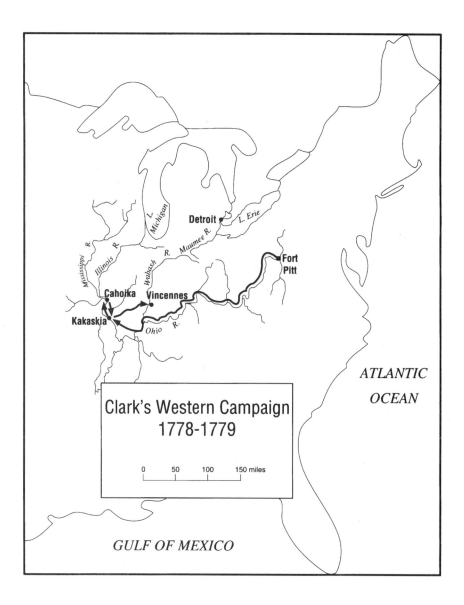

Clark's Western Campaign
1778-1779

0   50   100   150 miles

ATLANTIC
OCEAN

GULF OF MEXICO

In June 1778, Clark left with 200 men to attack the British. First by boat and then by trail, Clark led his men through the wilderness, sometimes going more than two days without any food.

He and his men first spotted the British at Fort Kaskaskia on July 4, 1778.

He organized the local trappers and traders who were French and ready to throw off any loyalty to the King of England. First he captured Kaskaskia, then Praire du Rochet, Cahokia, Vincennes (also known as Fort Sackville), all without the need of firing a single shot. Each British outpost fell to Clark and his men. He was clever and used the French trappers, who were friendly with the Indians, to persuade the Indians not fight against him. Had the Indians fought with the British, they would have defeated Major Clark.

The British Lieutenant Colonel Hamilton heard of the southern forts and supply posts which had been taken by Clark and prepared to attack Clark himself. Leaving in early October, Hamilton arrived at Vincennes in mid December. The local settlers, who before had promised loyalty to Clark and the American cause, now pledged their allegiance to England, and Hamilton recaptured the fort without a fight.

As the year drew to a close, Clark had reached the shores of the Mississippi River, over 180 miles to the west. He decided to turn around and attack Hamilton.

1779–1780 • A Traitor and the British Head South

☆☆☆☆☆☆☆☆☆☆☆☆☆☆☆☆☆☆☆☆☆☆☆☆

Marching in the dead of winter across the frozen wilderness, with fewer than the 200 men he started with, Clark planned his attack. Crossing frozen swamps and frozen trails, he reached Vincennes in February 1779.

When he arrived, he discovered that the British had no idea that his army was approaching and were unprepared for a winter attack. Clark captured one of the local settlers and told him to inform everyone who was loyal to the United States to stay in their homes. All others were to go to the fort for protection because he was going to recapture the fort. Letting the settlers believe his force was much greater than it was, he hoped to spread fear through the town and fort.

He then separated his men into small units and approached the fort from different directions. Each unit was told to make as much noise as possible and sound as though they were over a 1,000 men. His plan worked. Hearing the screams, many of the local settlers believed a huge army had arrived, and many joined Clark, wanting to be on the winning side.

Many of the Indians who were helping the British left the fort and a few joined the Americans. The American army swelled in size. The fort was well armed and supplied and had three artillery pieces in each corner of the fort. Hamilton ordered the artillery to fire when Clark's troops fired on the fort. All day long, as they prepared to fire their cannon, the British soldiers were picked off by Clark's men. Hamilton was unable to fire back. With no hope of winning, Hamilton surrendered. The most hated man on the frontier, British Lieutenant Colonel Hamilton, was captured, and the Americans secured the western frontier.

Even Thomas Jefferson, who was then the Governor of Virginia, wanted to treat Hamilton poorly because he had instigated so many vicious attacks against American settlers.

Clark continued fighting in the west through 1782. The Americans were able to hold onto Illinois even though the British still maintained some control in northwest Ohio and the Lake Erie area.

New York Becomes Critical   General Clinton in New York decided to try to establish a chain of fortified positions along the lower Hudson River Valley to protect the smaller unit kept in New York City. He wanted to control the area from West Point southward. In May 1779, Clinton moved 6,500 men towards the American fort at West Point, New York. Washington countered, moving his men north as well. The Kings Road, linking New England to the other colonies, had to be kept open.

On July 15, 1779, General Wayne attacked the British at Stony Point at night using bayonet only. He overwhelmed the British and captured the position. However, the Americans quit the position, believing it too costly to try to keep. Nonetheless, the effect of this attack was enormous. The American spirits were lifted and Clinton decided it was not worth it to move against West Point.

The value of West Point to both armies was great. Washington understood how it helped to protect the road linking the colonies together, while Clinton understood the need to separate the colonies by capturing West Point.

During the Saratoga campaign General Arnold was wounded in the leg during heavy fighting. After the victory was secured, he was sent to Philadelphia for medical care. While under treatment he grew restless and wanted to return to active duty. As time went on, he met and married Peggy Shippen, an outspoken supporter of Britain in this war.

Soon after his marriage, many members of Congress began to question his every move, even asking for a dollar accounting of the supplies he used and lost during battles. They demanded to know why he gave passes to people to move freely between British held New York and Philadelphia. Many no longer trusted him and they questioned his loyalties.

Major John André, under Clinton's command, saw an opportunity here. He had heard of the way Congress was now treating Arnold and he offered gold to Arnold and the rank of general in the British army if he would cooperate with the British, and General Clinton in particular. Arnold felt put upon by Congress and grew resentful and angry at not being returned to command. Pushed beyond what he accepted as tolerable, Arnold agreed to cooperate.

Together, André and Arnold devised codes and sent messages to each other. Nothing happened for a year and Major André gave up their connection.

Meanwhile, Washington was planning his next major offensive. He was going to meet the British on the New York frontier, along

Benedict Arnold *Due to feeling he was being unjustly treated by the Continental Congress, and by George Washington, Arnold decided to betray the American cause and turn the West Point Military Fort over to the British. His plan was spoiled before the British could take the fort, but he still became a general in the British army. Library of Congress*

the Mohawk Valley. In early 1779, Washington issued simple orders: invade the lands of the Six Nations, the Iroquois Indians, in western New York from Lake Ontario to Lake Erie and south down through the Catskill Mountains.

The Indians of the Six Nations lived in small settlements with permanent wooden homes and they cultivated the lands. They wandered less than other Indian tribes.

Washington split his army into two columns. General John Sullivan of Pennsylvania was to head the western column and the other was to be led by General James Clinton of New York. Sullivan was delayed and by June of 1779 had barely gotten started. Meanwhile, James Clinton moved his army north and began a western trek. As he marched through the territory, his men attacked and destroyed Indian settlements along the way.

In August 1779, the British, along with their Indians allies, laid a trap for the two units. The three American Generals, Clinton, Sullivan, and Dearborn were good generals and spotted the trap. Coordinating attacks, they encircled the British and Indians. With just three men lost to Sullivan, the American army inflicted heavy casualties on the British and the Indians.

After this action, neither this British army unit nor the Iroquois Indians were able to put up much resistance for the rest of the war. Seneca towns were then wiped out, as well as those of the Genesee Indians. The Six Iroquois Nations were pushed back past Niagara into British Canada. Washington had removed the Indian threat from western New York.

During the year that Major André and General Arnold had no contact, Arnold was questioned and harassed by Congress. Asking Washington for a command position, he felt as though he was being snubbed and ignored.

Then in July of 1780, Arnold proposed a plan to deliver West Point to the British. He demanded a lump sum payment and a dollar amount paid for each American captured. The haggling between Arnold and the British seemed to go on forever. Washington, unaware of any wrongdoing on Arnold's part, offered him command of the left wing of his army. This angered Arnold further since he wanted and felt he deserved full command at West Point. Now Arnold was angry and came to terms with Clinton.

Arnold was never very polite or nice to his officers and when he took Washington's left wing, all that changed. Everyone wondered what Arnold was up to. At Washington's headquarters, Arnold wanted information concerning American spies; information that was only supposed to be given to General Washington.

Suspicions grew when he gave orders to allow a John Anderson to pass freely between the British lines to the south and West Point. Anderson was searched and stopped. In his shoes were found diagram plans of West Point and a pass written by Arnold himself. Captured, John Anderson revealed himself to be Major André. Before Washington could get there, Arnold was told that a spy had been caught with plans to West Point and would be questioned. In an attempt to escape, Arnold acted as normal as possible. He proceeded to take a barge south to inspect positions. There he met a British ship on the Hudson River and revealed himself to its captain and went to New York City. He believed General Clinton would still be able to capture the fort with just his knowledge of the fort's defenses. In addition, the publicity about his defection would help the British cause.

Major André was hanged as a spy. Arnold received some money and was made a British brigadier general. Arnold had been a major general with the Americans and was in effect demoted. Washington was devastated by this betrayal, taking it as a personal insult.

The War Moves South   In late 1778, British troops disembarked at the mouth of the Savannah River in Georgia. London wanted the war to be over. Taking a page from Burgoyne's idea of splitting the colonies apart, London wanted the south separated from the other colonies. American General Robert Howe, of North Carolina, maneuvered his army of 1,000 men between the British troops on the river and those moving up from British Florida. In early 1779, he was badly defeated and his army scattered. The British took Savannah and then Augusta, Georgia.

Georgia was now under British control.

General Benjamin Lincoln of Massachusetts tried to organize some resistance to the British and assembled an army. He contacted French Admiral d'Estaing off the West Indies Coast and 6,000 French soldiers were brought to offer additional resistance to the British forces.

It took nearly one full year for the army to organize and challenge the British in Georgia. On September 12, 1779, Admiral d'Estaing arrived and unloaded 6,000 French soldiers north of Savannah. But instead of attacking the British, he delayed, giving the British time to fortify their positions.

General Lincoln was looked down upon by the French commander and was all but ignored by the French. Ignoring General Lincoln's suggestions, on October 9th the French attacked the British in a poorly executed plan. Over 800 French and American soldiers were killed, while fewer than 100 British were killed. Lincoln wanted to attack again under a different plan, but Admiral d'Estaing took his men and left for the French island of Martinique. Lincoln had to withdraw to Charleston, in South Carolina. With no real army to resist them, the British were now free to move throughout South Carolina.

The Road to Yorktown and Victory

☆☆☆☆☆☆☆☆☆☆☆☆☆☆☆☆☆☆☆☆☆☆☆☆

Hearing of the British victory in Georgia, General Henry Clinton in New York recalled the 3,000 men sitting in Newport, Rhode Island and decided now was the time to attack Charleston, South Carolina. He then planned to move north, through to Virginia.

In May 1780, Clinton and his army landed south of Charleston and prepared to attack. Fearing punishment from the British, the leaders of Charleston pressured Lincoln not to leave Charleston under any conditions. He prepared to defend the city.

The battle was a foregone conclusion. The British General Clinton had over 10,000 men to Lincoln's fewer than 5,000. While Lincoln remained in Charleston, the British captured the one remaining escape route that might have been used by the American forces. When the British drew a circle around the town, Lincoln was forced to surrender. All of the Revolutionary War leaders of South Carolina were captured with the exception of Governor John Rutledge. The American cause in the south was deeply hurt.

General Charles Cornwallis *Charles Cornwallis was the British General who led for the British the final major campaign of the American Revolution. After several months of combat through the southern states, Cornwallis was finally trapped at Yorktown, Virginia. There he surrendered to George Washington ending the Revolutionary War. Library of Congress*

Clinton sent General Cornwallis to take the rest of the state. At Camden, South Carolina, Cornwallis met the American army and defeated it. By August of 1780, a chain of forts was established to hold South Carolina and Georgia. The American cause looked bleak.

In June 1780, things looked good enough for General Clinton to return to New York and leave General Cornwallis in charge.

The Americans were busy developing a plan of their own. A force out of North Carolina was hoping to drive the British into the coastal swamps and cause them to become trapped and useless. General Horatio Gates was put in charge of this force. He moved south with about 3,000 men.

A battle was fought at Camden, South Carolina. Both the British and the Americans tried a surprise attack on the same night. In the heat and confusion, both were forced to withdraw. Reports said the British far outnumbered the Americans, but Gates refused to hear opinions from any of his generals and officers. He ordered an attack. The American army was routed when their lines broke. Only General deKalb was able to offer any resistance. But as the other units collapsed and no longer offered resistance to the British, the British concentrated more on deKalb and his lines. Then deKalb's men failed as well. Broken and scattered, the American soldiers made their way north to the North Carolina border.

Gates, regrouping the army, found he had less than 700 men, with no supplies, guns nor ammunition. The entire south was now open to the British. Cornwallis planned to take advantage. The British command decided the first step was to send their American prisoners to Charleston. While on route, they were attacked by a band of American militia that came out of the swamp, led by Colonel Francis Marion. His exploits against the British earned him the nickname of the "Swamp Fox." Marion had only seventeen men, but they came out against the British, making noise for fifty or more men frightening the British. Marion captured the British soldiers and freed the American prisoners.

Next the British command decided it was necessary to gain complete control over the Carolinas. To accomplish this, the British sent a unit of 1,000 men west. Against this trained unit, western frontiersmen moved to block them. Only 900 men in all, but all of them good fighting men.

They met the British at King's Mountain, which stretched across both Carolinas. Attacking the British in Indian fashion, the American frontiersmen wiped out the British soldiers. Only those who had been sent out to search for food in the woods survived the disaster. Now Cornwallis rethought his plans and decided to wait out the winter. For the moment the British were stopped.

Congress had Washington send Nathanael Greene to take command in the south. On December 12, 1780, General Greene took command of the American forces at Charlotte, North Carolina. Once he had arrived and met the troops, Greene saw a number of well tested officers who fought with him at Monmouth and other battles. He was going to use them and their experience more than Gates had done.

Among the officers Greene met was a Lieutenant Colonel Henry Lee (father of the future Civil War General Robert E Lee). Greene understood that Lee and Colonel Marion knew the areas he was about to fight in and wanted their opinions and knowledge. He decided to use Marion and his men as guerrilla bands, harassing the British, and their lines of communication and supply.

Greene was getting ready. The two armies were to meet at the foot of King's Mountain again. The Americans had developed a simple plan. Using half the army, they would quickly attack the British and then perform an orderly withdrawal from the battlefield. Breaking off action, they hoped to trick the British into believing that they were retreating. Once the British would begin to follow, the Americans would reform their battle lines on the hillside. As they moved up the hill, the other half of the army would be secretly waiting to attack the British army, which was following the Ameri-

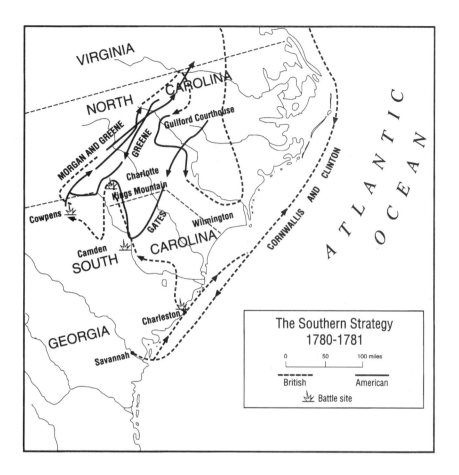

The Southern Strategy
1780-1781

cans. The retreating soldiers would suddenly turn upon the attacking British. Joined by the troops in hiding, they would be able to defeat the British.

Once the two armies clashed, the British commander Banastre Tarelton, ordered his men to follow and destroy the retreating forces. Instead, the retreating Americans turned on the British once they reached their fortified positions and reserve troops. The British were stunned. They tried to regroup but the Americans kept moving in on them in a circular action to push them down the hill. The

British were never given a chance to regroup. Many of the British threw down their arms while others fought on. Between casualties and prisoners, over 90% of the British force was lost. The Battle of the Cowpens was an American victory.

Cornwallis was surprised with the news of the loss at Cowpens. The British had the momentum going and could not afford to lose it. Cornwallis decided to pursue the American forces, catch them, and destroy them. It became a race to the Dan River. Could the British catch the Americans there before reinforcements could reach Greene?

The British matched the Americans move for move, never losing any distance between the two armies. Greene sent Colonel William Washington, a distant cousin of the Commander-in-Chief, with 700 men to slow down the British. The plan was to let the British find them, then head off to the north in the hope that the British army would follow them instead of pursuing the main army. Cornwallis did not fall for this trick. He pursued Greene.

Greene escaped to Virginia. The British now held the Carolinas and Georgia. A few of the rebel leaders such as Marion still operated in South Carolina, but the region was really controlled by the British.

Just south of Virginia, Cornwallis established his base of command. Offering pardons and good wishes to the people in the countryside, he hoped to win back many of the rebel sympathizers as he prepared for the spring offensive.

Meanwhile, Baron Von Steuben had been sent by George Washington to Virginia to help. Von Steuben was to oversee the defenses of Virginia and help prepare the army for battle. Greene's army now consisted of nearly 4,000 men and he hoped to draw Cornwallis into a battle along the Dan River. He had seen this spot during his escape from North Carolina and decided it offered good positions for his army. Now all Cornwallis had to do was accept the challenge.

Henry Lee's cavalry attacked the British lines and upset their field command. He established a firing line along a fence where they let go with several volleys of fire. In a fashion like that at Cowpens, the cavalry was to pull back to a more secure line and continue the fight. But the line behind Lee didn't hold. As the line broke, Colonel Washington's men moved forward, holding the line and forcing the advancing British line to waiver. British reinforcements moved forward to reinforce their line. As the battle raged on, the British line was beginning to falter but the sun was going down, forcing Greene to end the fight for the day. With the battle done, Cornwallis moved north.

Greene engaged the British at Camden, South Carolina. Victory was to elude him once again. It was not that he was not losing, he just was not winning. His plan to retake the south was not becoming the victory he expected.

Seeing his numbers diminish, Greene had Marion's guerrilla forces join the regular army for his next planned action. Just north of Charleston, Greene engaged the British army. In fierce fighting, both armies were severely hurt. Greene's troops pushed hard and broke the British lines, only to find stiffer resistance as they moved forward. Both armies had to break off the fighting as the casualties mounted. The British pulled back into Charleston, where they remained till the end of the war. Greene's army surrounded the city, keeping the British threat locked in.

Greene's plan to secure the south now seemed to be working.

Yorktown and Victory   In July 1780 French General Comte de Rochambeau arrived on the shores of Rhode Island with 5,000 regular French army soldiers. They were assigned to help fight the

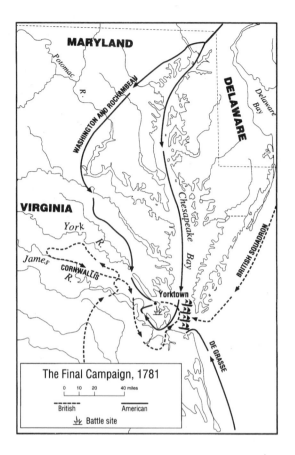

MARYLAND

Potomac R.

WASHINGTON AND ROCHAMBEAU

DELAWARE

Delaware Bay

VIRGINIA

York R.

James

CORNWALLIS R.

Chesapeake Bay

BRITISH SQUADRON

Yorktown

DE GRASSE

The Final Campaign, 1781

0 10 20   40 miles

- - - - British   ———— American

Battle site

British in America and not run off to the West Indies. It was what the American army needed. Washington was given the men and supplies he needed to continue the fight. But with delays of establishing the proper protocol for the two armies to work together, it was not until the next year that they were able to take any action.

The French had landed far from the fighting and Washington did not have the time to organize them for use along the Hudson River. He was also probably afraid that if the fine French troops saw the poorly equipped Americans, they would leave, believing the Americans could never win.

Meanwhile, British General Clinton decided to form a base of action off the Chesapeake Bay in Virginia. Using a lesson he had learned from the Americans, his troops were ordered to use hit and run tactics to hurt the Americans. General Benedict Arnold was assigned this task. In January 1781, Arnold landed and began to march through Virginia, going all the way to Richmond, the capitol of Virginia. Governor Thomas Jefferson could do little to help defend his state. Help was needed from elsewhere. Washington wanted to end the raids and capture the traitor Arnold. He sent Lafayette to do the job.

Lafayette moved south with 1,200 men under his command. The French fleet was ordered to back him up, but the British navy prevented this. Gathering Virginia militia and new recruits, Lafayette's command grew to over 3,000 men. He was now ready to do battle, and Cornwallis was ready to defeat him.

In late June, Lafayette received additional troops sent from Pennsylvania. With his forces strengthened, Lafayette was searching for action. By July, Cornwallis was moving north to engage him. The British were moving to the Yorktown Peninsula in Virginia. Cornwallis took his time trying to gain the best position before engaging the Americans. But before he could take any action, he received orders to send 3,000 of his men to New York City to help defend it. His numerical superiority was lost; the two armies were now equal in size.

With his army reduced in size, on July 6, 1781, the two armies began to engage in battle. Cornwallis held back a full attack, not knowing where Lafayette was with the main portion of the American forces. General Wayne, who recently joined Lafayette, was the first to engage the British. Unfortunately for him, he was to have his army destroyed with a British advance. Suddenly, Cornwallis turned and attacked Wayne's 900 men, who faltered and then

The Marquis de Lafayette *The Marquis de Lafayette of France came to serve in the Colonial Army. He asked for no pay or military rank. Instead, he asked only to serve in the cause of liberty. His actions in Virginia against the British General Cornwallis, allowed Washington to move colonial troops to Yorktown, Virginia, to finally trap the British army and cause their surrender. This military campaign ended the Revolutionary War. Library of Congress*

finally gave way. The British overran the American lines and the Battle of Greenspring Farm was a quick British victory. The two armies settled into the region and continued with small skirmishes.

On August 14, 1781, Washington received word that French Admiral de Grasse had left the French West Indies and was headed north to help him with more supplies and men. Washington decided to mass all his forces against Cornwallis and trap him in Virginia. In what must have seemed like an endless line of troop movement, the American and French forces crossed the Hudson River on the west bank and began to move southward. Generals Washington and Rochambeau kept their armies moving swiftly through New Jersey to Philadelphia and then still farther south. As they moved south, word reached Washington that de Grasse was in the Chesapeake Bay and 3,000 more troops were being unloaded.

The allied forces quickly marched south to meet with all the available troops. When all the forces joined, they reached a total of over 16,000 men ready to fight. The British army was going to be severely outnumbered.

On September 14th, Washington's combined army was prepared to do battle. Battle lines were drawn around the British camp. Trenches were dug and then filled with French and American troops. It became a slow siege, drawing closer, inch by inch, to the British defense. Firing from strong defensive positions, the lines drew a tightening circle around the British. Finally, Cornwallis was forced to give up his outer defenses lacking enough men to properly hold them. The Americans moved forward and occupied those positions.

One by one, each British supply route was cut off until Cornwallis was completely bottled up. With the French navy blocking a water escape route, Cornwallis and his army were trapped. In mid-October, in a night raid, Alexander Hamilton silently crept forward with his unit, attacked and captured entire British defense units before they had a chance to offer any resistance.

On October 17, 1781, Cornwallis, seeing it was useless to attempt to continue offering any resistance, asked for terms of surrender. On the 19th of October, the British came out from their positions and gave up their guns. The British agreed to surrender.

Cornwallis refused to surrender directly to Washington and had a second in command do the actual surrender. Washington responded by having a second in command act for him. The British soldiers marched out of their camp to the tune of an old British bar song, "The world turned upside down." They could not believe what had happened.

At that time, the victory at Yorktown was seen as a great victory but not "the great victory to end the war." Forces in other regions of the war were still poised to fight, though not much fighting occurred. Then in early 1782 the British withdrew from Savannah and Charleston in the south. Slowly it became known that the British were willing to negotiate a peace with American independence guaranteed.

Treaty of Paris   Negotiations dragged on. John Adams, Ben Franklin, and the other negotiators in Europe worked out a peace treaty to end the war with Britain. In the Treaty of Paris, Britain agreed to recognize the United States of America as a free and independent nation. Britain also agreed to grant the United States all the rights and privileges of an independent nation, including the removal of British soldiers from American soil.

The Treaty of Paris was the logical conclusion to the Declaration of Independence. Accepted in September 1783 by the negotiating team, the United States had only six months to approve and return the treaty to Britain. When it arrived in Philadelphia, Congress had only two short months to accept and return the treaty. The return journey across the Atlantic Ocean might take up to six weeks.

The United States of America was functioning under a set of laws known as the Articles of Confederation. These laws established a system which required a majority of at least nine states for any law or treaty to be passed.

Thomas Jefferson was then serving in Congress. He took it upon himself to make sure the treaty was signed and returned in the remaining available time.

Unfortunately for Jefferson, only seven states were in attendance in Congress. With at least nine needed to pass a treaty, Jefferson feared that all could be lost. He wrote to the delegations of the missing states, explaining the importance for the delegations to come at once. In January 1784, the delegations from Connecticut and New Jersey arrived in Philadelphia. With nine states represented, Congress voted and accepted the Treaty of Paris, officially ending the American Revolutionary War.

The Treaty was accepted and the United States of America was a free and independent nation.

Time Chart Study Guide of the American Revolution

1492	Columbus comes to the Americas and returns to Europe with his knowledge.
1607	The first permanent English colony established at Jamestown, Virginia.
1619	House of Burgesses established, first colonial legislature.
1620	Pilgrims come to America and create the Mayflower Compact, a written constitution.
1629	Economic hardships spread throughout England as a depression takes hold; many willing to come to the "new world."
1636	Hartford, Connecticut established with a written constitution, the Fundamental Orders, which expand rights of colonists.
1643	The New England Confederation of Colonies established. Massachusetts, Plymouth, Connecticut, New Haven and Rhode Island all agree to a mutual defense treaty from Indians.
1649	Toleration Act of Maryland; it allowed anyone who was Christian to obtain free land and a right to participate in the government.
1664	British take New York from the Dutch.

1660's	First Navigation Acts passed, used to regulate and control commerce between colonies and the mother country.
1696	Board of Trade established to control and oversee growth and development of the colonies.
1732	The last English colony of Georgia was established.
1702–1713	Queen Anne's War.
1740–1748	King George's War, the first European war to directly affect the American British colonies.
1754	Albany Plan, proposed by Benjamin Franklin; it suggested a loose union between the colonies for common defense. It was eventually rejected by all the colonies.
1754–1763	The French and Indian War, final conflict between the British and French on the North American continent.
	England wins the war and gains control of the eastern half of the continent and finds itself heavily in debt.
1763	Proclamation of 1763 which stopped new settlements in the west, restricted travel to the western territories, and required a license to trade with the Indians.
1764	Sugar Act places taxes on sugar, coffee, wines and other products imported into the American colonies. Colonists protest these taxes.
1765	House of Burgesses in Virginia writes a letter of protest to the King of England stating what they believe to be their rights as Englishmen.
	Sugar Act repealed and replaced with Stamp Act. Stamp Act placed a tax on newspapers, licenses and other legal documents.
	Sons of Liberty were formed and led protests against the taxes.
	Colonies gather to work together against the Stamp Act at the Stamp Act Congress.
	Stamp Act repealed as protests lead to violence in the colonies.

1765 *(cont.)*

Parliament passes a special law for the New York colony, requiring it to pay for provisions for the army no other colony was asked to pay for.

Quartering Act by Parliament required some colonists to have English soldiers live in their homes.

1766

Parliament removes the Stamp Act. While removing the Stamp Act, Parliament finds it necessary to pass the Declaratory Act, which said Parliament always had the right to tax the colonies. It expressed the idea that the colonies were subordinate to Parliament and Parliament could pass any law it wished to "bind the colonies and people of America."

1767

Townshend Acts placed taxes on glass, lead, paints, paper, and tea imported into the colonies.

1768

News of Townshend Act reaches the colonies which again protest Parliament's actions.

Lord Townshend replaced by Lord North as Prime Minister and Townshend taxes are quickly removed.

British troops arrive and remain in Boston, Massachusetts.

1769

House of Burgesses is disbanded by order of the Virginia Governor Botetcourt.

Former members of the disbanded legislature gather to organize a colonial boycott of English products.

The Committees of Correspondence established by Sam Adams. They were used to keep the lines of communication open between colonies.

1770

Boston Massacre—British soldiers, while on duty, fire into a crowd of citizens. Five colonists are killed. John Adams defends the accused soldiers.

1772

Citizens in Rhode Island board and set fire to the British navy vessel the *Gaspee,* after it has run aground. During the incident the captain of the ship is shot dead.

1773

Parliament passes the Tea Act, changing the way tea is imported into the American colonies. The East India Tea Company is given exclusive rights to import and trade tea in the colonies. Protests occur in all the colonies.

1773 *(cont.)*

In Boston Harbor, colonists dressed up as American Indians board the English ship, the *Dartmouth*, which is loaded with tea and dump the tea into the water. This becomes known as "The Boston Tea Party."

1774

Parliament passes a series of laws to punish Boston for its "Tea Party." In March 1774 Parliament passes three Coercive Acts. The first, the Port Act of 1774, closes Boston Harbor until the citizens of Boston pay for the destroyed tea. The second, the Administration of Justice Act, transfers criminal cases outside Massachusetts until the Governor determines that fair and impartial trials with honest convictions can be achieved. The third act, the Massachusetts Government Act, reorganizes the colony's charter.

A military governor, General Gage, is assigned to take control of the Massachusetts colony.

The colonies agree to meet in Philadelphia to discuss the problems they are having with Parliament. At this Continental Congress, the attending colonies agree to a boycott of English products and tell the citizens of Boston to arm themselves to resist tyranny.

1775

England sends word to General Gage to use military force if necessary to end the problems in Boston.

British march to Lexington and Concord to capture military supplies of American militias. En route, the British engage the militia in fighting.

British return to Boston where the colonial militia surround the town.

Fighting spreads as Fort Ticonderoga is captured from the British in New York.

George Washington is made Commander-in-chief of colonial forces as colonies join together to resist the British army.

During the Battle of Bunker Hill, the British are forced to withdraw as the American militia win the battle. American army attempts and fails to invade Canada and to win it to the American cause.

1776

British withdraw from Boston as the American forces push the British out of Boston.

General Washington takes command of forces in New York.

Continental Congress passes the Declaration of Independence as the colonies declare themselves to be a new free and independent nation, the United States of America.

1776 *(cont.)*

Washington defeated in New York.

Washington captures Trenton after crossing the frozen Delaware River on Christmas night.

1777

Washington takes troops and spends winter In Morristown, New Jersey.

Defeats in southern Pennsylvania and Delaware lead to British capture and occupation of Philadelphia.

In a major military campaign lasting several months, American General Gates defeats the British General Burgoyne at Saratoga, New York. Burgoyne's army surrenders.

1778

Because of the victory at Saratoga, New York, France agrees to recognize and support the United States of America.

Washington and the army suffer through a harsh winter at Valley Forge, Pennsylvania. During winter encampment, Baron Von Steuben trains the American army.

Washington defeats British in Battle of Monmouth.

Major Clark defeats the British on the western frontier and captures British Lieutenant Colonel Hamilton.

1779

American General Anthony Wayne defeats the British in lower New York and keeps the road open to the New England states.

American General Benedict Arnold is approached by British to betray the American cause.

American forces defeat Mohawk Indians and British in central and western New York state.

British embark on a new plan to divide the southern states from the ones farther north and invade Georgia and South Carolina.

1780

General Arnold betrays the Americans.

British have several victories in the south and gain control over Georgia and North and South Carolina.

1780 *(cont.)*

In July 1780 French General Comte de Rochambeau arrived on the shores of Rhode Island with 5,000 regular French Army soldiers.

British invade Virginia.

1781

Americans, led by French General Lafayette, defend Richmond, Virginia against British forces.

French Navy, under the leadership of French Admiral de Grasse, arrives off the coast of Virginia to assist in the trap for General Cornwallis.

American army traps British army in Yorktown, Virginia. General Cornwallis surrenders to the Americans in the last major battle of the Revolutionary War.

1783

Treaty of Paris signed granting independence to the United States of America. It is accepted by Congress in January 1784.

Important Individuals of the American Revolution

ADAMS, ABIGAIL   She was self-taught individual, who served as an important listener and source of ideas for her husband, John Adams. Together they would work through many of the early ideas of freedom and independence. In her own right, Abigail helped organize the Boston resistance while her husband served in the Second Continental Congress, reminding him "not to forget the women" as they go about preparing for a new nation. *Pages 79, 80*

ADAMS, JOHN   Adams was an early leader in the move to independence. Aligned with the Boston Radicals, Adams was an outspoken critic of the Massachusetts Governor. He defended, in court, the British soldiers accused of firing into the citizens of Boston (Boston Massacre). As a leading member of the Second Continental Congress, he led the fight for independence. After the passage of the Declaration of Independence, he was one of the few delegates who continued to serve in Congress to help organize a government for the new nation. Later, he was leading spokesman for a strong federal government. He served as the first vice president of the United States and later as its second president. *Pages 45, 56, 57, 58, 64, 65, 66, 78, 79, 80, 89, 91, 94, 140, 144*

ADAMS, SAMUEL   One of the earliest advocates for independence. He organized the Sons of Liberty, the Committees of Correspondence, and later with John Hancock, the Massachusetts Committees of Safety. Serving in the Second Continental Congress, he was an outspoken leader for independence. After the war, he became a leader against the organization of a federal government. Once the federal government was established, he served as Governor of Massachusetts. *Pages 34, 39, 40, 42, 44, 45, 48, 52, 54, 56, 63, 64, 65, 66, 73, 89, 144*

ALLEN, ETHAN   A Vermont militia leader who was key in the capture, early in the war, of Fort Ticonderoga. *Pages 77, 84*

ANDRÉ, MAJOR JOHN   The man who served as the go between the British army and Colonel Benedict Arnold. *Pages 124, 126, 127*

ARNOLD, BENEDICT   An American Colonel who betrayed the American cause by attempting the turn over the American Fort at West Point to the British. *Pages 77, 84, 85, 87, 112, 124, 126, 127, 137, 146*

BURGOYNE, GENERAL JOHN   A British General who devised a plan early in the American Revolution to attack the Continental Army, from Canada, separating New England from the other states. The poor support for his plan among other British generals fighting the war, led to its failure and his surrender at Saratoga, New York. *Pages 105, 109, 110, 111, 112, 113, 114, 127, 146*

CARLETON, GENERAL   A British officer who was defeated by General Arnold while the Continental forces made their way north to invade Canada. Fate allowed Carleton to yet be successful, when a message carried by an Indian from Arnold to American General Schuyler was instead handed over to him. Complete knowledge of the Americans' plans, led to a total British victory and the destruction of the American invading force. *Page 85*

CLARK, MAJOR GEORGE ROGERS   An American officer who led the campaign against the British in the western territories. It was his success that led to the defeat of the British in the West and the capture of Lieutenant Colonel Henry Hamilton, the most hated man on the western frontier. *Pages 119, 120, 121, 122, 123, 146*

CLINTON, GENERAL (SIR) HENRY   British officer who, for most of the war, was in control of the New York to Philadelphia region. Defeated by Washington in a head to head battle at Monmouth, New Jersey, Clinton then concentrated his efforts in New York City and lower New York State. Clinton was instrumental in causing Benedict Arnold to betray the American cause. *Pages 109, 117, 123, 124, 126, 127, 129, 130, 131, 137*

CLINTON, GENERAL JAMES   An American officer, who along with Generals Sullivan and Dearborn, defeated the British in western New York State. *Page 126*

CORNWALLIS, GENERAL (LORD) CHARLES   A British officer who led a successful campaign in the South against the American forces. In a few swift battles, he was able to defeat and capture the southern states. It was when he entered Virginia, that his fate was sealed. With nearly half his army ordered back to New York City, and opposed by Lafayette, he was eventually forced to make camp at Yorktown, Virginia. While there, Washington arrived with overwhelming numbers causing a siege of the British lines to begin. After several weeks of holding out against superior numbers, and after a defeat in a night attack, Cornwallis was forced to surrender the British army to Washington. This became the last major battle of the war. *Pages 101, 103, 104, 130, 131, 132, 134, 135, 137, 138, 139, 140, 147*

D'ESTAING, ADMIRAL   A French naval commander at the time of the American Revolution, arrived in South Carolina to assist the American forces. Instead of helping, he refused to listen to any American officer and led both armies into a series of defeats. After a short time on the American shores, d'Estaing withdrew his forces to the French West Indies. *Page 128*

DAWES, SAM   Along with Paul Revere and Dr. Samuel Prescott, set out on a midnight ride to warn the local militia that the British were on their way to Concord, Massachusetts to try to capture the arms and ammunition stored by colonial forces. *Page 74*

DEARBORN, GENERAL HENRY   An American officer, who along with Generals Sullivan and James Clinton, defeated the British in western New York State. *Page 126*

DICKINSON, JOHN   A writer and politician, who early in the conflict led the challenge to Parliament's attempts to tax the colonies. *Page 48*

FRANKLIN, BENJAMIN   Printer, writer, inventor, statesman, scientist, philosopher and politician, who was very involved all aspects of the American Revolution. An early proponent of cooperation among the thirteen colonies in events that would affect all the colonies. He served as the colonial representative, in London, to Parliament before the war. He was also a leader in the Continental Congress for the move to independence. After the war, he served as the American Ambassador to France and was a participant in the Constitutional Convention. *Pages 27, 35, 41, 58, 91, 140, 143*

GAGE, GENERAL THOMAS   The British officer sent by Parliament to take control of Boston in 1774. He established military rule over the colony. It was under his command and orders that the British set out to Concord, Massachusetts to capture the arms accumulated by the local militias. *Pages 65, 66, 73, 74, 145*

GATES, GENERAL HORATIO   An American officer who led the American forces in northern New York that defeated and caused the surrender of General Burgoyne and his British army. He was later sent by Washington to try to stop the British advance occurring in the Carolinas. Defeated by the British, he was able to regroup his men and offer a small and limited resistance to the British. *Pages 131, 132, 146*

GRASSE, ADMIRAL FRANCIOS JOSEPH PAUL DE   A French officer, who along with George Washington, blocked the escape route of the British from Yorktown, Virginia. Using his fleet to prevent British ships from entering Chesapeake Bay, de Grasse did not allow supplies to reach Cornwallis. At the same time he did not allow the army to escape. *Pages 138, 139, 147*

GREEN MOUNTAIN BOYS   A small group of Vermont militia, who captured the British Fort Ticonderoga for the American cause, early in the war. *Page 77*

GREENE, GENERAL NATHANAEL   An American officer, who was instrumental in saving the American army when the British moved northward towards Pennsylvania early in the war. Later, he was given command of the American forces in the South, in at attempt by Washington to stop or slow down the success of the British advance in the Carolinas. *Pages 106, 109, 132, 134, 135*

GRENVILLE, GEORGE   British Prime Minister in 1763 who first proposed taxing the American colonies to raise money to pay for the French and Indian War and to use to govern the colonies themselves. *Page 38*

HALE, NATHAN   An American spy caught and hanged by the British. *Page 99*

HAMILTON, CAPTAIN ALEXANDER   An American officer who served as the personal aide to Washington during the war. He led the final assault, at night, at Yorktown to defeat the British and force Cornwallis to surrender. After the war, he became a leading spokesperson for a federal government.

Later, he served as the first Secretary of the Treasury. He was killed in duel with Aaron Burr. *Pages 104, 118, 139*

HAMILTON, LIEUTENANT COLONEL HENRY   A British officer on the western frontier who organized the Indians to raid and attack colonial settlements, sending terror along the western settlers. Finally captured and imprisoned. *Pages 119, 121, 123, 146*

HANCOCK, JOHN   A leading colonial radical, who as a businessman, was able to help finance much of the colonial resistance in Boston. He was also one of the early leaders in the Sons of Liberty, Committees of Correspondence, and the Committees of Public Safety. He served as the President of the Continental Congress, where his fame grew as the man who signed the Declaration of Independence with a large bold signature. *Pages 54, 57, 58, 62, 66, 68, 73*

HENRY, PATRICK   One of the earliest colonial leaders to speak out and challenge the authority of English rule when he believed it to be wrong. As a great orator, he helped convince others to his cause by his powerful speeches. He had the honor to serve as the first Governor of Virginia when the war began. *Pages 35, 36, 44*

HOWE, ADMIRAL RICHARD   A British Naval officer who used his ships to prevent supplies from reaching the American army. *Page 88*

HOWE, GENERAL WILLIAM   A British army officer who commanded the British army from New York to New England. He defeated Washington on Long Island, and then forced him to flee from New York altogether. Again, he challenged and defeated Washington, only this time it was near Philadelphia, Pennsylvania. *Pages 88, 95, 97, 99, 100, 101, 105, 106, 108, 110, 111, 113*

HUTCHINSON, (LIEUTENANT) GOVERNOR THOMAS   Serving first as Lieutenant Governor then as Governor of Massachusetts, Hutchinson strongly opposed the radicals who challenged British authority. He tried his best to break up the radical groups in Boston. *Pages 42, 54, 56, 57, 58, 60, 62, 64, 65*

JEFFERSON, THOMAS   A scientist, philosopher, writer, farmer, and politician and an early outspoken critic of English rule over the colonies. His clear writings quickly moved him to the front of the colonial debates on freedom and independence. Author of the Declaration of Independence. Later, he served as Minister to France, first Secretary of State, vice president, and as the third president. He believed his greatest accomplishment was the establishment of the University if Virginia. *Pages 66, 67, 68, 89, 91, 92, 94, 123, 137, 141*

KING GEORGE III   The king of England. King George allowed his ministers to rule the colonies. It was by their mishandling of the situations that he lost the colonies in the war. *Pages 89, 92, 94*

KNOX, GENERAL HENRY   An American officer who functioned as a close personal aide to Washington. He was often strategic in winning battles with Washington. *Page 104*

LAFAYETTE, MARQUIS DE   A French nobleman who came to serve in the American cause for no pay. Impressed by his sincerity and skill, Washington made Lafayette an American general. It was Lafayette who was able to maneuver General Cornwallis into Yorktown. Once achieving this, he called for Washington and all the American forces to join him in Virginia to destroy the British army. *Pages 105, 117, 137, 147*

LEE, GENERAL CHARLES   An American officer who often found himself at odds with Washington. Washington finally removed him from command during the Battle of Monmouth in New Jersey. It was after Lee's debacle at this battle that the Continental Congress began to allow Washington to select his own officers. *Pages 99, 101, 116, 117, 118*

LEE, LIEUTENANT COLONEL HENRY   A key American officer who helped stop the British, late in the war, with their plan to control the South. *Pages 132, 135*

LEE, RICHARD HENRY   Served as one of the Virginia representatives to the Continental Congress. It was Lee who proposed to the Congress that the colonies declare their independence from England. *Page 68*

MARION, COLONEL FRANCIS   An American officer, who was also known as the Swamp Fox. An expert in the area of South Carolina, Marion and his guerrilla band of soldiers harassed and defeated the British army often. *Pages 131, 132, 134, 135*

MONTGOMERY, GENERAL RICHARD   An American officer, who along with General Philip Schuyler, led the colonial army on their invasion of Canada. Fate played a trick on Montgomery, as the British army was secretly given the invasion plans, by an Indian messenger. The British were prepared for the American army, which led to a major defeat and the destruction of the invading army. During the Battle of Montreal, Montgomery was killed. *Pages 78, 83, 85*

OTIS, JAMES   Early Massachusetts radical, who spoke out against Parliament's attempts to pass laws and taxes on the American colonies. *Pages 35, 39, 40, 44*

PICKERING, GENERAL TIMOTHY   During the campaign near Philadelphia, Pickering was instrumental in preventing the British army from destroying a portion of the Continental Army. *Page 108*

PRESCOTT, DR. SAMUEL   Along with Paul Revere and Samuel Dawes, set out on a midnight ride to warn the local militia that the British were on their way to Concord, Massachusetts to try to capture the arms and amuninition stored by colonial forces. *Page 74*

PRESTON, CAPTAIN THOMAS   The British officer in charge of the men who fired their weapons in the "Boston Massacre." During his trial, he was represented by John Adams as his lawyer. Through the testimony of eye witnesses, Adams proved the soldiers were forced into firing their weapons at the threat of their own safety. Found innocent he returned to England after the trial with the other seven soldiers. *Pages 53, 54, 56, 57*

REVERE, PAUL   Along with Dr. Samuel Prescott and Samuel Dawes, set out on a midnight ride to warn the local militia that the British were on their way to Concord, Massachusetts to try to capture the arms and ammunition stored by colonial forces. He was the only one of the three men to be captured. *Pages 64, 74*

ROCHAMBEAU, GENERAL COMPTE DE   A French general, who arrived in 1780 with men and supplies for Washington's army. Giving his full support to Washington, Rochambeau allowed him to march both armies into Yorktown, in northern Virginia, from New York State. This troop movement prevented the escape and ultimate defeat of General Cornwallis leading to the surrender of the British army and the end of the war. *Pages 135, 139, 147*

RODNEY, CESAER   An early and strong supporter of American independence in the Continental Congress. *Pages 44, 68*

RUTLEDGE, JOHN   An American political leader who reluctantly supported the move to independence. However, once it was passed, he supported the American cause to the fullest extent. *Pages 44, 68, 129*

SAMSON, DEBRA   One of many women who assisted the Continental Army in the fight for independence. Samson secretly dressed as a man to join the army and fight. *Page 80*

SCHUYLER, GENERAL PHILIP   An American officer, who along with General Richard Montgomery, led the Continental Army on their invasion of Canada. Fate played a trick on him, as an Indian messenger secretly gave the British army the entire plans for the invasion and which allowed them to be prepared for the American army. This knowledge led to a major defeat and the destruction of the invading American army. Schuyler was later instrumental in the British defeat and surrender in the Saratoga Campaign. *Pages 78, 83, 85, 110*

STARK, GENERAL JOHN   An American officer, who came with an army towards the end of the Saratoga Campaign and completely blocked any retreat General Burgoyne might have had. It was the final blow leading to the surrender of the British army at Saratoga. *Page 114*

STEUBEN, BARON VON   A Polish General, who came to help the American cause. Arriving at Valley Forge, Von Steuben shouted out commands, through an interpreter, at the American troops. Taking several months, he trained the army into a better fighting force. Towards the end of the war, he was important in the planning of the defense of Virginia. *Pages 116, 134, 146*

SULLIVAN, GENERAL JOHN   An American officer, who along with Generals Dearborn and James Clinton, defeated the British in western New York State. *Page 126*

TARELTON, COMMANDER BANASTRE   A British officer, who was severely defeated at The Battle of the Cowpens. Losing more than 90% of his army, Tarelton gave the Continental Army a major boost in its attempt to stop the British victory in the South. *Page 133*

TOWNSHEND, LORD   The British Prime Minister, who in 1767, had Parliament pass a series of taxes. The items taxed were as glass, lead, paints, paper and tea imported into the colonies, among other things. *Pages 48, 50, 144*

WASHINGTON, GENERAL GEORGE   An American officer, who early in the conflict with England proposed a boycott of English goods in to the Virginia colony. An outspoken critic of the British treatment of the colonies in Virginia's House of Burgesses, he was selected as one of the colony's representatives to the Continental Congress. He was selected by that congress to be Commander in Chief the Continental Army. From March 1775 to the end of the war, he was head of the Continental Army. He accepted General Cornwallis' surrender at Yorktown to end and win the war for the Americans. Later, he served as president of the Constitutional Convention. After the acceptance of the new constitution, he served as the first President of the United States under the Constitution. *Pages 29, 30, 31, 51, 68, 77, 78, 80, 82, 83, 84, 87, 88, 89, 95, 96, 97, 98, 99, 100, 101, 102, 103, 104, 105, 106, 108, 109, 114, 115, 116, 117, 118, 119, 123, 124, 125, 126, 127, 132, 134, 136, 137, 138, 139, 140, 145, 146*

WAYNE, GENERAL WAYNE   An American officer, who time and again prevented a defeat for Washington and the Continental Army. Was crucial in holding off the British army near Philadelphia as Washington regrouped his defeated army. Was a key player in the success of the American army in the Battle of Monmouth, and an important member of Lafayette's command team in the trapping of Cornwallis at Yorktown. *Pages 106, 108, 117, 123, 137, 146*

Glossary

"A Summary View of the Rights of British America"   A pamphlet of instructions, written by Thomas Jefferson, for the delegates from Virginia to the Continental Congress.

Boston Massacre   On March 5, 1770, after being taunted and attacked by citizens of Boston, in panic, seven British soldiers fired into the crowd. Five colonists were killed.

Boston Tea Party   On November 27, 1773 the British ship, the Dartmouth, while in dock, was boarded by colonists dressed as Indians. They proceeded to crack open all cargo of tea and dump it into Boston Harbor.

boycott   To refuse to buy or use the products or services of another country; used to show displeasure.

Coercive Acts   See Intolerable Acts

colonial   Having do to with the colonies or a specific colony. Ex: a colonial legislature was the lawmaking body of a specific colony.

colony   A group of people, or their descendants, who go from their own country to a new one and live together in a settlement or town under the control of the parent country.

Committees of Correspondence   Established by Sam Adams; they were used to keep the lines of communication open between colonies.

Continental Army   The army of the United States of America during the Revolutionary War.

"Declaration of Independence"   Written by Thomas Jefferson, it was an announcement from the Second Continental Congress to the world, stating the reasons and the justifications which the American colonies had in their attempt to break away from England and establish their own nation.

"Declaration of the Causes and Necessity for Taking Up Arms"   A pamphlet co-authored by John Dickinson and Thomas Jefferson. It attempted to justify to the world the need for the American colonies to offer unyielding resistance to the British. The pamphlet rejected independence; instead, it pleaded for a compromise which would bring the two sides together.

Declaratory Act   When Parliament removed the Stamp Act, it passed this act saying that Parliament always had right to tax colonies. It expressed the idea that the colonies were subordinate to Parliament and that it could pass any law it wished to "bind the colonies and people of America."

Gaspee   A British naval vessel which went aground while attempting to stop colonial smugglers. After learning of this, colonists from Rhode Island, boarded the ship and burnt it, but after they killed its captain.

House of Burgesses   The colonial legislature of the Virginia colony.

Intolerable Acts   In March 1774 Parliament passed three Coercive Acts in response to the Boston Tea Party. They were called intolerable by the colonists. The first, the Port Act of 1774, closed Boston Harbor until the citizens of Boston paid for the destroyed tea. The second, the Administration of Justice Act, transferred criminal cases outside of Massachusetts until the Governor determined that fair and impartial trials with honest convictions could be achieved. The third act, the Massachusetts Government Act, reorganized the colony's charter. It made the office of the Governor more powerful, causing the local town meetings to be of little authority. It now had the state council appointed instead of elected, and finally it altered the method of jury selection when trials were to be resumed.

intolerant   Not willing to recognize or respect others' beliefs or practices.

legislature A group of people empowered to make laws for a country or state.

Mercantilism An economic system that declared a nation's wealth was measured by its ability to supply all of its own needs.

minutemen Local militiamen who were ready to fight with extremely short notice.

Navigation Acts Beginning in 1663. Parliament passed a series of laws to try to control trade with its colonies. These laws required that all goods shipped to or from the colonies to anywhere, must first pass through an English port. This allowed Parliament to tax foreign goods to attempt to force the colonists to buy only English products.

Parliament The legislature of Great Britain.

Proclamation of 1763 At the end of the French and Indian War, England was faced with a huge debt. In order to limit the amount of troops it would need on the western frontier, England agreed to the Indian demand that settlers not be allowed to move west. In return, England expected peace along the western border.

Quartering Act Even before the last protest against the Stamp Act had occurred, Parliament saw fit to pass the Quartering Act. This law required the colonists to house and feed new British troops who were being sent to colonies. This only occurred in a few of the colonies, but many of the leaders of the colonies were afraid that this was the beginning of an English conspiracy to take away their rights as Englishmen.

siege A slow encirclement of a fortified position by an opposing army intending to take it.

six-weekers Men who agreed to serve in the army for a period of only six weeks. At times, men joined to fight for 3 month or month periods as well.

Sons of Liberty Groups which had been organized to protest British taxes. Begun by Sam Adams in Massachusetts, they were led by many of the more violent and radical protest leaders.

Stamp Act of 1765   To replace the Sugar which it had just repealed, Parliament passed the Stamp Act. It raised money by taxing newspapers, legal documents and licenses. This is the way taxes were collected in England and Parliament believed the colonies could not object to being treated just like other Englishmen. Unlike the Sugar Act, the Stamp Tax was a direct tax on the colonists themselves and not on products imported.

Stamp Act Congress   In October of 1765, the colonies were asked to send representatives to New York to meet and discuss the Stamp Act and the problems it caused. The meeting in New York, produced a series of resolutions of protest. They declared Parliament had no right to interfere with the colonies. They went further than just the Stamp Act, saying Parliament had no authority to tax or eliminate trial by jury as it had done in some colonies. They declared for the first time that the colonists should think of themselves as Americans, not as Virginians or New Yorkers. By November 1, 1765, when the Stamp Act was to have gone into effect, Americans boycotted anything which would require a stamp as the Congress suggested.

Sugar Act of 1764   This law placed taxes on sugar, coffee, wines and other products imported into colonies. It was the first time that Parliament tried to raise taxes in the American colonies.

Tea Act   In the spring of 1773, Parliament changed the rules for tea trade. It gave the East India Tea Company the exclusive right to import tea into the colonies. In addition, Parliament also passed a tax on the tea. In revamping the tea import system, the cost of tea, including the new tax, would be lower than it had ever been before.

Townshend Acts   In June 1767, Parliament passed a series of taxes for the American colonies called the Townshend Acts. Proposed by Prime Minister Lord Townshend, these laws placed taxes on glass, lead, paints, paper and tea imported to the colonies. They also included a special provision suspending or prohibiting meetings of the New York legislature for not spending additional money for the British soldiers in that colony to buy salt, vinegar, cider or beer.

veto   The power to prevent or prohibit a proposed law or act.

Bibliography

Alden, John Richard. *The American Revolution 1775–1783*; Harper Torchbooks—The University Press, Harper & Row, Publishers, New York, 1954.

Atlas of American History; Rand McNally, Skokie, Illinois, 1991.

Boorstin, Daniel J. *The Colonial Experience*; Random House, Inc., New York, 1958.

Cunningham, Noble E. Jr. *In Pursuit of Reason: The Life of Thomas Jefferson*; Louisiana State University Press, Baton Rouge, 1987.

Ferling, John. *John Adams: A Life*; The University of Tennessee Press, Knoxville, 1992.

Freeman, Douglas Southall. *Washington*; Charles Scribners' Sons, New York, 1985.

Garraty, John A. *The American Nation*; The American Heritage Publishing Company, New York, 1966.

Jensen, Merrill, ed. *Tracts of the American Revolution 1763–1776*; The Bobbs-Merrill Company, Inc., Indianapolis, 1967.

Lancaster, Bruce. *The American Revolution*; Houghton Mifflin Company, New York 1971.

Langguth, A. J. *Patriots: The Men Who Started The American Revolution*; Simon and Schuster, New York 1988.

Morison, Samuel Elliot. *Sources and Documents illustration the American Revolution and the Formation of the Federal Constitution*; edited by:, Oxford University Press, New York, 1965.

West Point Atlas of American Wars; Frederick Praeger, Inc., New York, New York, 1945.

Wheeler, Richard. *Voices of 1776*; Penguin Group, New York, 1991.

Index

DISCARD

DATE DUE

DISCARD